WE SPEAK AS LIBERATORS
Young Black Poets

WE SPEAK
AS LIBERATORS
Young Black Poets

An Anthology Edited with an
Introduction by ORDE COOMBS

DODD, MEAD & COMPANY · NEW YORK

COPYRIGHT © 1970 BY ORDE COOMBS

ISBN 0-396-06211-3
Library of Congress Catalog Card Number: 78-114241
Printed in the United States of America
by The Cornwall Press, Inc., Cornwall, N. Y.

Thanks are due to the following for permission to reprint the material indicated: S. E. Anderson: for "Junglegrave." Desirée A. Barnwell: for "Will the Real Black People Please Stand." Richard W. Baron Publishing Co., Inc.: for "After the Rain," "The Revelation" from AIN'T NO AMBULANCES FOR NO NIGGUHS TONIGHT by Stanley Crouch, Copyright © 1970 by Stanley Crouch. Joseph Bevans Bush: for "Nittygritty." Pearl Cleage: for "Responsive Reading," "Confession," "Glimpse," "Retrospect," "Untitled," "For Death by Choice," "Feelings of a Very Light Negro as the Confrontation Approaches." Corinth Books, Inc.: for "Dancing All Alone," "Dance for Militant Dilettantes" by Al Young, Copyright © 1969 by Al Young. Jayne Cortez: for "How Long Has Trane Been Gone?" "For Real," "Bull Shit." Lawrence S. Cumberbatch: for "I Swear to You That Ship Never Sunk in Middle-Passage!" "Again the Summoning," "In the Early Morning Breeze," "Fake-Out." Walter K. Dancy: for "Jazz Coltrane Sings." Jackie Earley: for ". . . to be a woman." Entertainment Management, Inc.: for "Some Brothers Cry" by Alan Weeks. Mari Evans: for "Vive Noir!" "I Am Not Lazy . . . ," "Speak the Truth to the People." Lanon A. Fenner, Jr.: for "A Sweet Thing/Last Thoughts." Wally Ford: for "Sunrise on the Sunset," "Dry Wishing Well." Janice Marie Gadsden: for "We Don't Need No Music," "Everything." Paula Giddings: for "Death Motion," "Rebirth," "Resurrection." Nikki Giovanni: for "The Great Pax Whitie" from BLACK JUDGEMENT, Copyright © 1968 by Nikki Giovanni; "Poem (No Name No. 3)" from BLACK FEELING BLACK TALK, Copyright © 1969 by Nikki Giovanni. Clayton E. Goss: for "And If I Die Before I Wake," Copyright © 1970 by Clayton Goss. Linda Goss: for "Revolution Man Black," Copyright © 1969 by Linda Goss. Donald Green: for "Truth," "Growing Clean," "Making It, or Black Corruption."

R. Ernest Holmes: for "Black Lady in an Afro Hairdo Cheers for Cassius," "Black Woman," "Two From the Country." The Ron Hobbs Literary Agency: for "Riding Across John Lee's Finger," "All Praise," "Blues, For Sallie," "Sallie Jewel" by Stanley Crouch. Alicia L. Johnson: for "Monologue." Charles Johnson: for "crossed legs," "the parking lot world of sergeant pepper." Herschell Johnson: for "To Mareta," "We Are Not Mantan." Alice H. Jones: for "For Sapphire, My Sister." Arnold Kemp: for "A Black Cop's Communion," "Guilt Redeemed," "How to Succeed," "Hello Blackness," "The End of the World," "Love Me Black Woman." Leyland King: for "I could never ask you," "Didn't it come on like a tidal wave." Jewel Latimore (Johari Amini): for "Masque," "Utopia" from BLACK ESSENCE by Jewel Latimore, Third World Press, Chicago, 1968. Don L. Lee: for "Re-Act for Action" from THINK BLACK by Don L. Lee; "In the Interest of Black Salvation" from BLACK PRIDE by Don L. Lee, Broadside Press, Detroit. Tena L. Lockett: for "The Almost Revolutionist." James R. Lucas: for "The Beat." Bob Maxey: for "Moses Miles," "blues," "The City Enscriber." Don A. Mizell: for "I Want You To Hear Me," "Hope was faced alone." A. X. Nicholas: for "This Baptism with Fire . . ." "(For Lee)," "(For Mack)," "(For Poki)." Raymond R. Patterson: for "Invitation" from 26 WAYS OF LOOKING AT A BLACK MAN, Award Books, Copyright © 1969 by Raymond R. Patterson. Arthur Pfister: for "The Poet's Guilt," "If She Bees," "If Beer Cans Were Bullets," "Ode to the Idiots." Herbert Lee Pitts: for "Reality," "We Must Lead." Timothy L. Porter: for "Now in the Black," Copyright © 1970 by Timothy L. Porter. Eric Priestley: "Poetry," "Recreation." T. L. Robinson: for "Twang." Carolyn M. Rodgers (Imani): for "Newark, For Now (68)," "A Non Poem about Vietnam or (Try Black)," "Eulogy," "U Name This One," "Jesus Was Crucified or It Must Be Deep." Sonia Sanchez: for "right on: white america." Ruby C. Saunders: for "Lawd, Dese Colored Chillum," "Don't Pay," "Be Natural, Baby," "The Generation Gap," "My Man Was Here Today," "Auditions." Johnie Scott: for "A Short Poem for Frustrated Poets," "What Poetry is for Me," "Poem for Joyce." Saundra Sharp: for "Reaching Back," "Seeing Eye-Dog" from THE WINDOWS OF MY MIND by Saundra Sharp, Copyright © 1970 by Saundra Sharp/Togetherness Productions. Dan Simmons: for "Nationalism." Shirley Staples: for "Getting It Together," "A Sister Speaks of Rapping." Glenn Stokes: for "Blue Texarkana." Robert L. Terrell: for "For Frantz Fanon." Charles Thomas: for "In Search of a God," "Ode to the Smiths: Bessie, Mamie, Laura, Clara, and Trixie." James W. Thompson: for "Arms & Exit," "Beauty Then is Being," "Mock Pop Forsooth: a tale of life and death." Quincy Troupe: for "A Splib Odyssey," "A Day in the Life of a Poet," "Flies on Shit," "The Wait," "Dirge." Raymond Turner (The People's Poet): for "Buttons," "Find a Role, Define a Role." Jacques Wakefield: for "it ain't no jive," "our world is—," "well well—ma ace boo coo." Dell Washington: for "Learning Family." Wender & Associates: for "I Arrive in Madrid," "Dancing on the Shore," "For Poets," "Moon-Watching by Lake Chapala," "The Move Continuing" by Al Young. Michyle White: for "I prepare for night changes." Art Wilson: for "Treasure Hunt," "Black Sunrise."

For Kerston and Claer and Kae

CONTENTS

ix

INTRODUCTION

When I was asked to consider compiling an anthology on the works of new, generally unpublished, black poets, I immediately thought: "No, not another anthology." There has been, over the past few years, such a plethora of hastily assembled anthologies that one has been forced to wonder just what editors and publishers have in mind. Why the hasty collections? What was being proved? Or disproved? Did the anthologists really see a new phase dawning? Did they see the fantastic growth of the black man's belief in the efficacy of THE WORD? Well, yes and no. BLACK FIRE did. Others did not.

Then I decided to look at all the extant material and I saw the necessity of doing what has now been done: the assemblage of works of infrequently published blacks who came of age—literally and psychologically—during the horrendous American sixties. For it was clear to me that we were faced with a generation of black writers who had decided that, at whatever cost, they would psychologically liberate themselves from the altar of white supremacy, and having done so they would liberate their brothers.

Who are these young men and women who have seen Selma, have wept in Mississippi and New York and Denver? Who are these people who now, throwing off the pain of adolescence, have begun to speak in the sweeping language of revolutionaries? Who, I wondered, are these Americans who with unremitting candor denounce what the American system has done to their brothers, but like heroes will not seek exile? Well, they are the same smart and bright-eyed people who, in 1954, had seemed to their parents to be standing on the threshold of a new age. They were to be deceived, of course, and their parents were to continue, in the face of terrifying odds, quietly to affirm their humanity, to furnish their children with sinews until those children could loudly proclaim their own liberation.

It is not easy to see how they came about. How these young people, in the morass that surrounds them, achieved the toughness to throw down the gauntlet and to announce that whatever "freeing" of their peoples' minds there was to be done, they would do it. It is an act of colossal arrogance to assume that one knows more than one's elders. But every day we see, again and again, that these young giants are right, that they not only know more than we do, but are willing to pay the price to know even more.

If there is one moment that galvanized these heroes, it was when Stokley Carmichael, on Mississippi's dusty roads, announced that what black men needed was BLACK POWER. BLACK POWER. It is not fashionable now to praise Carmichael, but I have no doubt that his vociferousness will be remembered, and many black people, who for whatever nebulous reasons denounce him today, will praise him tomorrow. It was his voice that reverberated, that picked up the sound waves from Douglass and Dubois and Malcolm and put into words what a generation was feeling. And the celebration of oneself is only the beginning. After Birmingham and Watts and Newark, after 1954 and 1963 and 1968, the lyricists turned inward, not in defeat, but in celebration of what was always there and what in the haste to assert one's Americanness, one had forgotten to examine. Yes, one was BLACKBLACK-BLACK. And this was a message and a song. This was worth talking about, in bars, in schools, in funky basements and in jails. It was worth talking about because for so long one had not been sure that it was a subject worthy of mention.

Now throughout this sometimes tortured, torturing country, there are many young black men and women who have decided that they will fashion a language for themselves, that when they write, they will write for their peers and for those people whose dues have paid their way. Michael Thelwell, in a profound piece for *Ramparts,* October 1969, states that: "It is difficult to set down the rhythms and cadences of black language, or to reduce to the written word the passion, ecstasy and intensity that flows through the language and music of a storefront church meeting or movement rally. Difficult, but not impossible." It is precisely to that difficulty that these writers have addressed themselves, and at the core of this anthology is the belief of these blacks that they will use the distinctive language—the linguistic forms if you will—of their communities to define themselves. And they will do this ON THEIR OWN TERMS. How liberating, then, are the love songs of Pearl Cleage, the lawyer-poet R. Ernest Holmes's celebration of the street women of Harlem, Jacques Wakefield's insistence that "the world is us now," Arnold Kemp's apocalyptic shout that it is "The End of the World." And always in this collection one finds the sustained passion, the uncompromising necessity to affirm, to safeguard, a dignity so long denied. And the blackness, always the blackness, always the attempt to turn what was once negative into a sharpening rod of creativity.

It will be noticed that established names such as Don L. Lee, Mari Evans, Carolyn Rogers, and Nikki Giovanni appear. These poets are still young and modest and brilliant. They may oppose my calling them "established," but they will be hard put to deny the effect they have had on the other poets whose works appear in this collection. It was they, really, who forced many black poets to ask their colleges by what yardstick they were to be considered educated. And having forged their identities— painfully and at great cost—they compelled others to finely chisel theirs. The poet Shirley Staples in *Getting It Together* says it all. [She had to awaken from her] "dream world of reactionary flowers," when the

> WEEDS
> of Don Lee, Ameer Baraka, Giovanni, Pfister,
> and others made
> my rose petals wither.

It has been my contention, for some time now, that American blacks have been the only group of non-Caucasians to decide to eradicate the symbols of white psychological rule that have emblazoned the earth. American blacks, despised and poor, with only minor tools at their disposal, have set out to defeat racism on its most affluent ground. It is precisely this hoped-for defeat that thrusts young blacks into a syndrome, more arduous and exciting than most of us realize. Since blacks have decided to free themselves, then they must decide how to fashion that freedom. Nothing must be inviolate. The past that has been offered us is a dim miasma of lies and distortions. But it is precisely to that past that these champions return. It is through that research that they ascertain what was truth and so shout about it. And it is here, too, that they find the genesis of the lies that were cruelly meant to keep us—forever—in psychological bondage.

The voices of black poets are hardly raised in unison— and that is as it should be. One does not need artistic infallibility, one can do without the spectacle of a coterie of sycophants around a leader, or an extended club of mutual self-congratulatory members. On the need to fashion a new world, a relevant one for black people, a more humane one for black people, there is no dissent. And these black artists are up to the task. I do not think I overstate my case when I say that the assertiveness, the grandeur of a new generation determined to call the bully's bluff, find roots in the artist's call for victory.

And I think, too, of the praise these artists bestow on their mothers and fathers, who saw it all, and took it and fashioned champions. It is in that unsentimental glance at the past, and the reaffirmation that our common experience has made us all brothers and sisters that the strength of the future lies. Ruby Saunders * knows this; she thinks there can never be a generation gap among black people, and she calls upon young blacks to consider that even though:

> . . . the white folks calls you news.
> Remember . . . Tom . . . and . . . Aunt Jemima
> Bent low to pay your dues.

The liberation of black peoples' minds from the vise of whiteness must be one of the struggles of the seventies. This liberation has not greatly touched Africa, hardly touched the West Indies, and has only begun to soothe the ravaged souls of American blacks. It is the young black

* See p. 163 (Saunders).

artist who must insist on this liberation; who must carry
that message throughout the non-Caucasian world; who
must reiterate to Europeanized and befuddled blacks in
Africa and in the Western ambit that real freedom is not
the ability to speak French like Frenchmen or wear Eng-
lish judicial wigs. It is this artist who must—now that he
has begun to reclaim his life—speak in the loving, angry,
grandiose voice of the liberator.

ORDE COOMBS—E.S.C.

S. E. ANDERSON

Junglegrave

Send me no flowers, for they will die before they leave
    America
Send me home, no matter how far strewn I am across this
        rice-filled land
Send me home, man, send me home   even if I am
    headless
                                    or faceless
keep my casket open and my grave uncovered
for I want to show my brothers that it is their blackskin that
            stops them from being as free as whites
That white see blackskin and say we are the fodder of
    America
                                the Libertine
Send me no flowers, for my grave that I was born in
My Mother died one more death when I was stillborn:
    alive & black
My Race was still and stagnant with grief of my birth

Vietnam: land of yellow and black genocide . . .

Send the President my flowers cremated and scented with
    the odors
of my brothers' napalmed flesh and my sisters' bombed-out
    skulls

Send me no flowers, man, send me no flowers

DESIRÉE A. BARNWELL

Will the Real Black People Please Stand

Will the real black people please stand:
Whose forefathers worked this land together,
Whose heritage is undated,
Whose pride remains uplifted;
Undaunted by the white man's statistics,
Pushed forward by initiative,
Unstilled by useless chatter.

Is this us:
Whose cooperation we dare not trust,
Irresponsible to past assignments,
Content to beat around the bush?
Stand up, black people . . .
Dressed in polka-dot shirts and striped ties,
Flowered, and possessed by *them*.
Is this really us?

Will the real black people please stand:
Those fearless of the unconventional,
Moved towards their own blackness,
Prone to influence and set trends,
Schooled in *their* times and folkways,
Dedicated to worthwhile endeavors,
Attentive to meaningful expression.

Is this us:
Uncommitted to work, driven to pleasure,

2

Preoccupied with semantics,
Hung up on ego projection,
Fooled by long talkers who say nothing,
Harassed by uncontrolled belligerence,
Cynical to the point of madness.
Is this really us?

Will the real black people please ACT.

JOSEPH BEVANS BUSH

Nittygritty
(*To Everett LeRoi Jones—Meditative Man*)

We all gonna stop sliding stuff, tighten
Up, stop locking Black asses and start
Locking Black arms, hearts and souls.
We all gonna come from behind those
Wigs and start to stop using those
Standards of beauty which can never
Be a frame for our reference; wash
That excess grease out of our hair,
Come out of that bleach bag and get
Into something meaningful to us as
Nonwhite people—Black people.
We all gonna grab the minds of our
Children, make them vomit up the
Super white patriotism fed them
In the public schools as history
And inform them that: "We are beautiful
People with African imaginations";
That we are descendent from killers
Of lions and builders of pyramids
And not cotton-picking niggers.
We all gonna see that we are afflicted
By the white landlords, merchants, tavern
owners, etc., who infest our communities
And devise ways and means to get rid of

4

This affliction and get our own
Thing going.
We all gonna see that moving
Out of the ghetto merely solves
The problems of our immediate
Families and does not begin to
Alter the plight of the larger
Black family;
That our salvation lies in
Transformation, not integration:
Changing our areas from dark dungeons
Of despair to bright valleys of hope.
We all gonna start thinking
In terms of total protection
And preparing ourselves for the
Third World; realizing that
We are "struggling with depraved
Eagles" who, having a horrible history
Of mass murder and inflicting pain,
Will stop at nothing to destroy us.
All of this is to say: throat-
Cutting time is drawing nigh and
We all gonna be ready.

PEARL CLEAGE

Responsive Reading

If we say it here
in this rat-filled hallway,
will it be the same?
Grease and prints of
forgotten fingers parade down the walls.
If our lips form the words
will they be swallowed up in
shouted curses
and approaching sirens?
Will they splinter and fly—
clinging stickily to the dead
brown ceiling and
absorbing the smells and sounds
and sadness?
I will say it—
at least let me determine
why I will shed tears.
You must say it after me.
Don't wait!
Quickly before it is lost
and swallowed and gone
Quickly—
        I love you.

Confession

If I lie naked
with my gloves
folded
on the table,
my lips parted,
do not think it is
true
that I love you.
I still wear my
hat.

Glimpse

i saw you
on my walk last
night
you were running
between the
neatdark rows of
pine trees
behind the house
and even though
your mouth was
open
you made no sound.
your lips were stretched like
rubber
over your teeth

but your sound
was shaking inside
you
and never reached me
through the muffling skin.
i saw you
last night and
the red drops on your shirt
and the bloodprint of
your hand upon the trees.
i saw you
on my walk last
night.
Running.

Retrospect

Old woman—
I can see you
huddled in your
window
remembering now ancient
lovers
who are as withered
as you.
Wrapped tightly in
your shawl
your eyes no longer look

out
but only peer in.
The fragile gold frames
of your dusty glasses
are almost a shield
but not quite
and every once in a while
I can see you shiver
in a space between
memories.

Untitled

My feet
are rooted in a
poison lake.
The muck squeezes
between
my toes
and pulls me down.
The blood-red waters
lap against my legs
and take skin away
in every wave.
Every ripple I make
destroys me
and stillness only
aids the steadily pulling
mud.

The clams have
ringed me
and they are slimily content
to ooze and wait;
their filthy white blobs
creeping hungrily
between the parted
lips
of their
shit-brown shells.
And wearily,
I am waiting too.
Standing alone in the
swirling water;
watching my face
in the crimson
concentric circles
of my struggle.

For Death by Choice

From where the sun
has stopped above
me,
I stand and
bare my breasts
to the sky and offer you
myself.
The taste of his

betrayal
is still on my lips,
but that is my
only imperfection
as I come to you
in sunlight and in silence.
The mound of my
belly
is soft and smooth.
My thighs
are firm and strong.
I have made my
choice
and I know you will be
faithful.
While there is still
time,
I spread my legs
and offer you
myself.

Feelings of a Very Light Negro
as the Confrontation Approaches

When it comes
(and make no mistake—
    it's coming)
which way will I go?

Whose bullet will send
my life
choking and bubbling
up from my chest into the filth
of some unknown,
but silently waiting, street?
My pale skin and
        thin lips
alienate me from my
people.
They are suspicious of
my claim to
        blackness.
They gaze into my pale
blue eyes
and they know that I have
never danced
        naked and gleaming with sweat
under a velvet African sky.
But my soul screams
against an alliance with
        you.
I am Black inside myself
and I hate you,
        for with your whiteness
and your power
you have destroyed me.

JAYNE CORTEZ

How Long Has Trane Been Gone?

Tell me about the good things
you clappin & laughin
Will you remember
or will you forget
Forget about the good things
like Blues & Jazz being black
Yeah black music
all about you

And the musicians that
write & play about you
A black brother groanin
A black sister moanin
and beautiful black children
ragged under-fed laughin
not knowin
Will you remember their names
or do they have no names
No lives—only products
to be used when you wanta
dance fuck & cry

You takin—they givin
You livin—they creating
starving dying trying
to make a better tomorrow

giving you & your children
a history
But what do you care about
history—Black history
and John Coltrane
NO
All you wanta do
is pat your foot
sip a drink & pretend
with your head bobbin up & down
What do you care about acoustics
bad microphones or out of tune pianos
and noise
You, the club owners & disc jockeys
made a deal didn't you
A deal about Black Music
& you really don't give
a shit long as you take

There was a time
when KGFJ played all black music
from Bird to Johnny Ace
on show after show
but what happened
I'll tell you what happened
They divided black music
doubled the money
and left us split again
is what happened

John Coltrane dead
and some of you

have yet to hear him play

How long how long has that Trane been gone

And how many more Tranes will go
before you understand your life
John Coltrane who had the whole of
life wrapped up in B flat
John Coltrane like Malcolm
true image of black masculinity

Now tell me about the good things
I'm tellin you about
John Coltrane
A name that should ring
throughout the projects mothers
Mothers with sons
who need John Coltrane
need the warm arm of his music
like words from a father
words of comfort
words of Africa
words of welcome

How long how long has that Trane been gone

John palpitating love notes
in a lost-found Nation
within a Nation
His music resounding
discovery
signed   Always
John Coltrane

Rip those dead white people off
your walls Black people
black people whose walls
should be a hall
A Black Hall of Fame
so our children will know
will know & be proud
Proud to say I'm from Parker City, Coltrane City,
    Ornette City,
Pharaoh City living on Holiday street next to James Brown
    Park in
the State of Malcolm

How long
How long will it take for you to understand
that Trane been gone
riding in a portable radio
next to your son lonely
Who walks walks walks into nothing
No City No State No Home No Nothing
How long how long have black people been gone

For Real

Holes in my arms
gone gangrene
Roaches spilling from my ears
on rats chewing the remains
of a bastard I killed with

a hair pin up my womb.

Purplemouth
Bubblemouth
                    Death
You are ugly
You are white
Death you are death.
No more uh uhnnn
don't touch me

I'm on my way to Mecca
Elijah in my head
A Panther in my eye
                    Love Lives
and I wanta taste myself inside
Mmmmmmmmm that pure nigguh pain
I don't feel strange
I hate the welfare line.

Call me fool
call me negro
call me any old goddam thing you want
                    assassinating mouth
                    trying to assassinate me
But I'll survive the night
my gold tooth a lighthouse keeping death away

I'll sink shame
& beat my wings
I've killed fear
& my soul's on fire
I confess

I am armed & prepared
to reproduce the love that made me live
I confess that this beautiful Nigguh is ready.

Bull Shit

bullshit bullshit bullshit
talkin' bullshit
as you learn from the devil how to exploit your brother and
wear your sister's dress—chump
talkin about power
why you black white freak
sniffing psychodelic panties of psychodelic bitches hiding
    out in
a psychodelic slum talkin about cul-ture
when you know that your mind was manufactured by
        motorola you
kodak color baboon screamin about revolution this and
counter revolution that and the only revolution you know is
lickin hairs off the devils ass & jackin off on television
talkin about you underground
aint that a bitch
on television talkin' about you underground
when the only underground you know is
riding those underground trains in that underground
        subway trying
to get to that underground job—punk
talkin about you a leader?

when you can't even lead yourself to the toilet to flush
    your mouth
shit lip motha fucka
you better come to yourself & get it together before
scott tissue rubs your guerrilla warfare out.

Riding Across John Lee's Finger

(For Walter Lowe)

The Blues meant Swiss-Up
way back when
then later it meant
another thing,
a change up of tears
from the suppressed loneliness
that glittered from our slick heads
to a more blatant tragedy:
the one we now call a natural,
the Blues billowed and sprouting
over our heads now,
nappy bent turned tears
and a scream for another place
as the maroon pants are replaced
with equally loud African clothes:
Though nobody, still, knows my name.

2.

My name is not from another place
my name is from here right now
and if I am a woman
my name may be Future Mae
and if I am a man
my name may be L.C. or W.B.

whatever my name is
whatever my way is
it is not from some place else
and I know now with my gold teeth
or the meat hanging from my arms
that makes me look like a huge bird
or my bangs combed all the way to the back of my head
behind Murray's
and I know now, forty years old,
riding a bicycle decorated with roses & white dolls,
know as I do the deacon shuffle in front of the pulpit
know the slow dance, baby, know the slow dance
like a crawlin king snake
raised straight up into a giant
walkin the water if it rains
know right now, slow dance, baby,
know right now
if I stood any taller
the stars would burn my hair off,
know right here that I am beautiful.
As if history didn't even exist
and don't need nothin
except how I am:
Cause that's where the future was.
Slow dance, baby:
A timeless state of mind.

All Praise

Get out of the way of my dignity.
You cannot give it to me
                        not when spools
of spooks are the harbors
of the golden threads
of spirits
not when sometimes we've lain
in the park
or stuck our fingers through the diamonds
of metal fences
on the climb to steal cumquats
Not when my woman
is the mother lode of poems
growing through the sickness
of this white earth,
                        this cadillac-filled
and seven-storied ice trays of Alaska
you call architecture
when you cannot even slant stones
toward the sky without engines
and blue prints
They, the pyramids, stand there
and the
broad-nosed lioness of the sphinx
laughs at your archaeologists

Get out of the way of my dignity.
Or the golden leaves of my fists
will split your heads.
                        The snow man
will melt.

His water
will dry.

And the people will dance tunnels
through the earth,
making the sun duck
and blink at their
brightness.
As Salaam Alaikum.

Blues, For Sallie

Eyes rolled open this morning
Eyes rolled, they opened,
run around the walls

Gone, that man, gone.

Now just give me somethin
to sip on
Now just give me somethin to sip,
sit by the window with.

Round rain on the pillows
shines white when the sun goes
to hide its bright ass behind the hills
Round rain on the pillows:
Sad-eyed Black Snake don't
crawl around in the bed no mo.

Sallie Jewel

Looking at the high-raised mini creations
of this green snake world and thinking
of those particular thighs, the glowing
brown yellow gold black of the Afro-Asian East
conjoined in the luminous softness of my Lady
who is so much farther than a hop away,
who writes me letters drained of all their dryness,
slick with her tears, but whose song rises crys-
tal delicate, doodle bug delicate under the sole
of a city where beasts file down their horns
daily, wrap or bob their tails before putting
on their suits or dresses and blow forth
smoke whether or not they have cigarettes—
there she is kneaded and ground as though she were corn
meal in a stone bowl, the stone bowl which is lariated
and thrown aside by her love as the delicate jiggle of
her heart rings
against the shit-covered corners & buildings of this city
a ringing song that grows as the circles of a target board
and sends my memory galloping to her face when a man
mentions a woman he saw, beautiful, wearing a hat.
Could she be beautiful, *actually* beautiful,
and not be my brown and brown and tender Ju Ju Jewel?

After the Rain

John's words were the words
Bird and the other winged creatures
sang:
> How the darkness could
> and would someday
> sink behind the sun,
> how we, when we grew
> to ourselves, past what we were,
> how we would dance outside
> bucking the eyes of all stars and all light
> how we would be as gentle
> as the rebuilt wings of a broken sparrow,
> how we would lick back the rain
> and wash ourselves with light
> and our eyes would meet His
> our God, our Om, our Allah, our Brahman.
> And we, like all oceans,
> would know
> and love each other.
> Salaam.

The Revelation
(*For John Coltrane*)

To tremble in prayer and trepidation
To tremble against trepidation in prayer
Screech   Scream   Cry
To tremble in prayer against trepidation

Screech-screech   Holler   Cry   Scream
To tremble with prayer
and arch the muscles of my back
in face of trepidation,
transparent beads bubbling from my forehead
     SCREECH   CRY:
Bird of blood with razor-sharp wings of boiling
stone fallen from God into my throat
claws my tonsils and sticks its feet
way down into my stomach
and I double over trying to vomit
forth this bird
to the rhythms of anklets ashake
in the dance of a black—blue-black
blue-black a black blue-black African Witch Doctor
wailing wailing—
scream high out into God,
fall heavily from the pole
of light He offers to the snow
of doubt that freezes
all Spiritual Feeling
to slabs of ice across the tongue:
Father, Father, understand me
Maker, Purification, Psalm of Warmth within Light
understand the reverent screams
of this confused devotee:
My journey like the invisible belt of the equator
that divides the world has been long,
the prongs of pain like an acne of lava
have raised their tips within my heart

I have lain high with the stone hips of Satan
crushing my head, weighing my thoughts
as though magnetized to gigantic boulders
falling in the hot hole of hell,
of wherever all these demons
like oceans of flies buzzed and chased me
stuck to me like flying needles to a pin cushion
but I saw
as my eyelids tearing from my face
and flapping away
like bats before
dissolving into Pure Light
the trajectory of Your Footsteps scarring the darkness,
the Most Merciful
Power with the
heavy-feathered
wings of wind
lifting my eyes
and I saw
I saw
I saw:
The scum peel back from the sky
and Your Force swell nature with such a light
that my tears boiled my whole body
and I exploded upward
sizzling the air
as an agony too powerful for this fever blister of flesh!

LAWRENCE S. CUMBERBATCH

I Swear to You, That Ship Never Sunk in Middle-Passage!

Tugging at containment
    all yields for the sake of bursting feet
        scuffling in the furrowed yesterdays

Inn beyond "the man's" whirl,
    funky dark as the hovel,

us children never sink
dancing on the water of futility

Never,

        never

Tomorrow is for the planters.

Plantation people dance at the Harlem Inn, Winstonville, Mississippi.

Again the Summoning

in new romance with blackness
burst the thread of last words
off the tangled spool
    where glare
    too many pictured kingdoms

painting bullets a missile
        girdled by noble goals
the heroic fabric of soulful minds
weaves thru
            imagined jungles
to a boogaloo party
of rainbow chiefs
       where beauty whimpers of exhaustion
       and the melody soon ends.

In the Early Morning Breeze

In the early crystal morning
       of glass-shattered streets
where the breeze has no challenge
       to weathered breasts
as of bahing sheep
gingerly as the leaf
           fall a thousand times
never to ground
I to no line
       remember ethiopia
    clothed in her tattered loin cloth
of popes' and bishops'
and longshoremen's kisses
         wispily sailing
from deep-water departure piers.

Fake-Out

When

spit, bombs
bits and pieces
of churches, homes
and unshackled, unfree people
make dull your shameless self

Then

mock our dreary hell
in a sunlit land

with all the white views
fit to print
about all the shameful people
unsunlit
look at demon others
and together radiate glee
at dying-off blacks
cried out me

Oh

but when rules are read
and they realize
white games aren't for us to win

maybe blacks dying-off blacks
will pick up bits and pieces
and start home again.

After Malcolm X, one of many died-off blacks.

WALTER K. DANCY

Jazz Coltrane Sings

Like one of my professors said to me
some hep cat with soul in his pen or type should write
a jazz
po
em o
baby don't you weep cause
I's here and the
music of Train is
blowing
showing all
the colors spread in OM
with Expression crying a
LOVE Supreme on screeching
Meditations
Chim Chim Chreeing over
Nature Boy's last solo
while Elvin is sweating over
Bessie's Blues
he can't get away from the
Father
the Son and
all are Holy with the Ghost
singing A Love Supreme and
doing Dahomey's Dance
can you hear

can you hear
can you hear
the real McCoy
Tyner touching those ivory keys
and Train

Train is blowing all the colors in OM
saying
MOM HOME WOMB TOMB soon like
a crazy spiritual fly away home

Train is gone
             gone
                  gone
                          baby don't you weep

like he's paying dues for us all
when he sings

        A LOVE SUPREME
        a love supreme
        a love supreme

        a love supreme

JACKIE EARLEY

. . . . to be a woman

To be a woman in the world as it was
I came
Giving birth to a black lifestyle.

I came
Snappin my fingers
Shakin my butt
Changin my mind
Pokin my lips
Suckin my teeth
Takin my time
Rollin my eyes
Draggin my feet
Talkin loud
Runnin my mouth
Being cute
Walkin proud

I came
Giving birth to a black lifestyle.
To be a woman in the world as it is
I still

Snap my fingers
Shake my butt
Change my mind
Smile most times

Suck my teeth
Use my time
Eyes straight ahead
Feet picked up
Talkin mellow
Talkin smooth
Being wise
Lowered my evil
Raised my pride

I'm here
Giving birth to a black lifestyle.
Come get your positive blackness
Let it soak through your positive mind

MARI EVANS

Vive Noir!

i
am going to rise
en masse
from Inner City

                  sick
                     of newyork ghettos
                   chicago tenements
              l a's slums

weary
        of exhausted lands
        sagging privies
        saying yessur yessah
        yesSir
        in an assortment
        of geographical dialects i
have seen my last
broken down plantation
even from a distance
                 i
will load all my goods
in '50 Chevy pickups '53
Fords fly United and '66
caddys I
        have packed in
        the old man and the old lady and

wiped the children's noses
I'm tired
of hand me downs
shut me ups
pin me ins
keep me outs
messing me over have
just had it
baby
from
you . . .
i'm
gonna spread out
over America
intrude
my proud blackness
all
over the place
i have wrested wheat fields
from forests
turned rivers
from their courses
leveled mountains
at a word
festooned the land with
bridges
gemlike
on filaments of steel
moved
glistening towers of Babel in place

sweated a whole
civilization
    now
                    i'm
gonna breathe fire
through flaming nostrils BURN
    a place for

          me
in the skyscrapers and the
schoolrooms on the green
lawns and the white
beaches
                i'm
gonna wear the robes and
sit on the benches
make the rules and make
the arrests say who can and who can't
              baby you don't stand
              a
              chance

i'm

    gonna put black angels
in all the books and a black
Christchild in Mary's arms i'm
gonna make black bunnies black
fairies black santas black
nursery rhymes and
              black
ice cream

i'm
gonna make it a
crime
to be anything BUT black
pass the coppertone
gonna make white
a twentyfourhour
lifetime
J.O.B.
an' when all the coppertone's gone . . . ?

I Am Not Lazy . . .

living
is
too much
effort . . .
I
am not
lazy . . .
just
battered . . .
I
cannot make
the
valiant push
the
all-for-God-and-
country

the good old college
try . . .
one
bullet . . . now.
this
coup-de-grâce is
such a small thing
and so
kind . . .

I am not
lazy . . . . . just
. . . battered.

Speak the Truth to the People

Speak the truth to the people.
Talk sense to the people.
Free them with reason.
Free them with honesty.
Free the people with Love and Courage and Care for
        their Being.
Spare them the fantasy.
Fantasy enslaves.
A slave is enslaved.
Can be enslaved by unwisdom.
Can be enslaved by black unwisdom.
Can be re-enslaved while in flight from the enemy.
Can be enslaved by his brother whom he loves.

His brother whom he trusts.
His brother with the loud voice.
And the unwisdom.
Speak the truth to the people.
It is not necessary to green the heart.
Only to identify the enemy.
It is not necessary to blow the mind.
Only to free the mind.
To identify the enemy is to free the mind.
A free mind has no need to scream.
A free mind is ready for other things.
To BUILD black schools
To BUILD black children
To BUILD black minds
To BUILD black love
To BUILD black impregnability
To BUILD a strong black nation
To BUILD.
Speak the truth to the people.
Spare them the opium of devil-hate.
They need no trips on honky-chants.
Move them instead to a BLACK ONENESS.
A black strength which will defend its own
Needing no cacophany of screams for activation.
A black strength which attacks the laws
exposes the lies disassembles the structure
and ravages the very foundation of evil.
Speak the truth to the people
To identify the enemy is to free the mind.
Free the mind of the people.
Speak to the mind of the people
Speak Truth.

LANON A. FENNER, JR.

A Sweet Thing/ Last Thoughts

She painfully holds back a Fart/To
the subway people she makes proud her
synthetic hair/chemically treated/smelling
of insecurity/ she perfumes HER/SELF
with bloomingdales expensive odors/ two
ounce Jars of massed-produced toilet
water/ Ten dollars to the bottle/ The
cheap brain washing process/ Her finger-
nails shine false color/ hair glimmering
with false straightness/ skin faded to a
Jive hue/ Body Blocked by "casual Polka-
Dots and a hip Bra"/ she is fooled by what
the mirror reflects/ She is a reflection of
a reflection/ imitator of the east-side
scenes Vogue-Bazarre Bullshit/ Her diet
of western bowel movement has stripped
her soul of meaning/ meaning to be white
she plays the Jive party scene until the
Bougaloo bacardi leaves her legs at right
angles in the back seat of Pacheco's car/
contemplating the half/ASS orgasm—
She smells each Finger—Looking for a clue
as she rides the subway back to the
roots of the Problem.

WALLY FORD

Sunrise on the Sunset

We had a pearl, a jewel that was ours
The fruit of hope, the search of our souls,
Then something flashed and it was no more,
Only the taste of ashes . . .
And the sunrise on the sunset of our love.

And the sun will rise on the sunset of our love.

It doesn't seem real, you going away,
I would beg and plead, but you know I won't.
So you walk and so do I,
In the sunlight that comes,
The brightness that comes,
From the sunrise on the sunset of our love.

I call your name in my mind
And I don't even hear it
But I know we loved while the moon did shine
And now happiness seems so far away.
As far as the sunrise on the sunset of our love.
As far as the sunrise on the sunset of our love.

Dry Wishing Well

There are times when I wish I could poet a poem.
I mean really—

Something so very beautiful
Enough to make the stars shine in your eyes
Or the music dance in your ears.
But now is not the time.
And that's really too bad . . .

But if I could
I would sing to you of the joys of loving
And probably shed a dry silent tear over the pain of losing.
Too bad, because I would tell of being
                          Black and Proud and
                          Black and Loud and
                          Black and Bowed and
                          Black and niggerdead.
What a gas we are—high or low
                  straight or sober
                  militant or just soft-shoein' along.

I wish I could tell of the warm sunshine of life in little
      babies' eyes
Or write the sound of a mother's love.
Or maybe just tell a little of the tracks that Trane trails in
      my mind.
I should be able to write the look of softness in a woman's
      eye,
Or the ice-fire love-hate that will make us free.
I wish I could.
I only wish I could.

JANICE MARIE GADSDEN

We Don't Need No Music

We don't need no music
We don't need no music
We got a rhythm   a beat
A syncopated   titallating
Way of walking   way of talking
Unh.
We don't need no music
We don't need no music
We're born to a beat
We live to a beat
We work to a beat
We love to a beat
Unnhh . . .
We die to a beat.
The great white metronome
Is tick tock tick tock
Ticking off the seconds
Ticking off the seconds
Ticking off the seconds
Of our lives—tick, tock
Unh
Strangulation   mutilation
Scarification mummification
Of young black minds
Of young black minds

But we don't need no music
We don't need no music
We got a rhythm   a beat
A syncopated   titallating
Way of walking   way of talking
Way of killing little white things
That tick tock tick tock
By superimposing our own
    black beat unh,
UNH!

Everything

Niggers and spics and assorted what nots
Black people   brown people   tan people
Has beens and will be's and various have nots
Walking up and down round black town
Lotsa jive jigaboos with dizzy dames
Downtown darky clowns and conked head hicks
        wearing tight pants showing
            ALL of what they've got, yeah
And everybody, everything got rhythm
Even the car horns have rhythm
    They all seem to be singing in an endless refrain
    BEEP BEEP AHH   BEEP BEEP AHH
Big bad black boogies wearing dirty old clothes
        a three day old beard and a weeks layer of dirt
Fantastically funny little faggots twitching along
        in tailored clothes and frilly shirts

Lotsa sisters, all kinds of sisters
Big fat mamas with 50 pounds of chest
    and 60 pounds of hips not to mention
    100 pounds of waist in between
Tall slim brown skinned young fawns
       wearing the latest styles and fried hair
Big bad bitches wearing cons, loud talking
    and fighting and fussing and cussing
Assorted hoes anything, anywhere, anytime
Pseudoblack brothers with natural heads
      and processed minds
Hustlers in dashikis who swear everything
    is fine
Everything is fine
Everything is fine
If you got a jones
If you drink wine
Everything is

    Here I stand
    With a blade in my hand
    Wondering if I should kill The Man
    He's blond, he's bright
    He's white, he's right
    Everything that I should like to be like
    Everything that I hate, all I despise
    Everything.

Everything is

    Standing on the corner stoned out of my mind
    Me, my pals and maryjane, ahh we knows we's fine
    Tearing up the road in my El D

Finally passing up the gray shadow
      that's always haunting me

Everything is
    everything, baby

    dying every morning
        from yesterdays wounds
    going out to the battlefront every afternoon
    dead every evening, almost
    and every night
        every night resenting the fact that
        you've got to start dying and dying and dying
        all over again tomorrow . . .
Everything is
    everything, baby
Which is nothing.

PAULA GIDDINGS

Death Motion

We're still dancing . . .

to
the nigger aberrations
of
our past/unpassed—

Tippin' lightly . . .

over
the skeletal screams
of
prophets who died
alone—

Movin' jim . . .

across
the immigrant's
broken tongue
tryin' to sell us
ourselves—

Struttin' jack . . .

past
the outstretched arms
of
yr women

mutterin' somethin' about
forbidden
fruit—

We're still dancin' . . .
to
the cheers of the
animals—
not even stoppin' to ask why

they are quietly building cages—

Rebirth

You reached in to pull my mind out of the mire of four
    centuries to tell me
                I am beautiful

You recast my heroes—
Garvey
DuBois
Malcolm

And draped them in the robes of prophets.
I am called sister and now you want to protect and write
    poems about me.
But what I don't understand about my new beauty is . . .
Why is it not reflected in your eyes?

Resurrection

I'm just trying to get next to myself,
To match up the center of my soul
With the center of just one star
To extend my arms and legs with four points
And my head with the one reaching for infinity . . .

But I knew others like that
Who became pinned to the sky/white stakes through their
    navels/
      squirming in an abandoned universe/blinding them by
      distant lights/spinning and spinning into meaningless
      masses of heat/

But it will be different this time . . .
    Malcolm, Marcus, Martin
It will be different . . .
    Trane, Billie, Bobbie
It will be . . .
    Richard, Langston

Because we are

And the Universe will be lighted by a
florescent sign,
"Under New Management"

NIKKI GIOVANNI

The Great Pax Whitie

In the beginning was the word
and the word was
Death
And the word was nigger
And the word was death to all niggers
And the word was death to all life
And the word was death to all

peace be still

The genesis was life
The genesis was death
In the genesis of death
Was the genesis of war

be still peace be still

In the name of peace
They waged the wars

Ain't they got no shame

In the name of peace
Lot's wife is now a product of the morton company

Nah, they ain't got no shame

Noah packing his wife and children up for a holiday
row row row your boat

But why'd you leave the unicorns, noah?
Huh? why'd you leave them
While our Black Madonna stood there
Eighteen feet high holding Him in her arms
Listening to the rumblings of peace
be still   be still

CAN I GET A WITNESS? WITNESS? WITNESS?
He wanted to know
And peter only asked who is that dude
Who is that Black Dude
Looks like a troublemaker to me
And the foundations of the mighty mighty
Ro Man Cat holic church were laid
peace be still
hallelujah jesus
Nah, they ain't got no shame

Cause they killed the carthaginians
in the great appian way
And they killed the moors
"to civilize a nation"
and they just killed the earth
and blew out the sun
in the name of god
whose genesis was white
and war wooed god
and america was born
where war became peace
and genocide is patriotism
and honor is a happy slave
cause all god's chillin need rhythm

and glory hallelujah why can't peace be still

The great emancipator was a bigot
ain't they got no shame
And making the world safe for democracy
were twenty million slaves
nah, they ain't got no shame

and they barbecued six million
to raise the price of beef
and crossed the 16th parallel
to control the price of rice

ain't we never gonna see the light

And champagne was shipped out of the east
while kosher pork was introduced
to africa
only the torch can show the way

In the beginning was the deed

And the deed was death

And the honkies are getting confused

Peace be still

So the great white prince
was shot like a nigger in texas
And our Black shining prince was murdered
like that thug in his cathedral
While our nigger in memphis
was shot like their prince in dallas
and my lord ain't we never gonna see the light

The rumblings of this peace must be stilled
be still   be still

Ahhh Black people
ain't we got no shame?

Poem (No Name No. 3)

The Black Revolution is passing you bye
negroes
Anne Frank didn't put cheese and bread away for you
Because she knew it would be different this time
The naziboots don't march this year
Won't march next year
Won't come to pick you up in a
honka honka VW bus
So don't wait for that
negroes
They already got Malcolm
They already got LeRoi
They already strapped a harness on Rap
They already pulled Stokely's teeth
They already here if you can hear properly
negroes
Didn't you hear them when 40 thousand indians died from
exposure to
honkies
Didn't you hear them when viet children died from
exposure to napalm

Can't you hear them when arab women die from exposure
to israelijews
You hear them while you die from exposure to wine and
poverty programs
If you hear properly
negroes
Tomorrow was too late to properly arm yourself
See can you do an improper job now
See can you do now something, anything, but move now
negro
If the Black Revolution passes you bye its for damned sure
the whi-te reaction to it won't

CLAY GOSS

And If I Die Before I Wake
(*Part of A One Act Play*)

Late at night I have heard the
    heat come on
        and go off into my dreams
to warm me
    cold and hot
together sometimes
        I have felt the stars shine through
the blinds and breathe the
chilly blue air speaking through
        the storm glass windows
warm hot together sometimes
    pyramids enter my mind
        becoming me and all my
friends dressed in Arab clothing
        snorting cocaine in a
        back room apt. building
Roman soldiers stinging my back with
    whips shouting at me to
        stop daydreaming and pick
        up another stone
        Zulus piercing their ears
while Nubian women masturbate
    secretly in their huts
        children being born bleeding

passages from the Bible called
   Fairy Tales for pious faggots
who insert corks up their rubberized
   assholes praying for a fart
     warm hot together sometimes (like)
candles sing and whisper memories of
my grandfather drunk on Saturdays
     straight on Sundays holding my
hand on a BusStop heading for Bethle-Ham
and Potato Salad Cabarets
     The Preachers wife fell out
and died of a stroke and the whole
   congregation cried
      the whole Congregation cried
   making analogies in their minds on
     how the Christman must have
     tried and failed and spoke and
      was jailed like Martin King
    a couple of years before the Sanitation
     workers strike
      warm hot together sometimes
     like a rooster who pees with an
    aluminum dick made in Tennessee
      forgetting to crow in the Morning
      forgetting to crow in the Morning
      forgetting to crow in the Morning
   letting everyone on the farm sleep an
      hour later
    milk turning to butter right
there in the cows five tities
    while the Cup ran away with the Spoon

while the Cup ran away with the Spoon
of Methedrene gold dust
white as snow and 18 inches deep
40 days you'll get no sleep
40 days you'll get no sleep
and drop alive at the end of
the week praying to a Junkie for
more warm hot sometimes together
messages from the Meditator Sun who
rises an hour later in the West
yawning and very tired himself
of the way things have been going
the way things have been going
He don't want to shine
He don't want to shine and
make people blacker and sadder and
blacker and madder and
blacker and badder and
blacker and blacker and blacker
poor rich together sometimes
warm hot together people
Dead alive together people staying awake at
night wondering about the 12 o'clock lunch
break whistle
will it ever break
will it ever break for
God's sake will it ever
become an antiquated fossil found
by some future archeologist
named Sanghay or Mali or Ghana
Dick Gregory laughing at you or

Dick Gregory laughing at you performing
            for him in the concentration camps
                ovens its so hot for Brothers
        like Africa used to be before they
            took us away
                Before they took us away and told
            us to go to sleep
                    tomorrow was the New World
                with old houses for the talented tenth and
                    project dungeons for the lower rents
                warm hot together sometimes happy
                dead-alive together sometimes sad
                    hoping that Rooster won't fuck up again
                    won't fuck up again
                        For God's sake Brothers
                            don't mess up again
like the House trained Niggers
        who turned in Denmark Vessey
    or the warm hot blood that
        oozed out of Bessie
                Didn't she say the blues Yawl
                Didn't she say the blues Yawl
    weren't you proud of that fat
        black sister who sang with
            all her heart until she
        died
                Didn't you cry brothers
                Didn't you cry brothers
            and go to bed with honky thoughts
        in your heads

Evil thoughts in your heads
turning over and over till
         Dinah came on the scene and
ain't Aretha mean as anything
with a truthful mouth singing
         warm hot sometimes dead alive
soul songs played on bargain store
         stereos loud and clear like
The forgotten tear
         of Emmett Till's Mother
         hoping that rooster will fuck up again
and give you and me and all of
                  us time
         Just a little time to get our
thing together and rise up warm
         hot together sometimes one unsuspecting
         morning like the Sun. AMEN.

LINDA GOSS

Revolution Man Black

Revolution Man Black
Listen, listen in my poem
of love song
Song of making babies
Sons to a battle
Daughters to make sons to a battle.

Revolution Man Black
Before you go
and win the battle
plant in me a seed
your son
your daughter to produce a grandson.

Revolution Man Black
while you are gone
winning the battle
I will feed our son
your ways of politics and love
our child will know Black Truth.

Revolution Man Black
when you come home
winning the battle
you will see you in our son
and you will plant more seeds in me
To make brave warriors and fertile daughters.

DONALD GREEN

Truth

Come away from them.
Empty your heads of
Their gadgets.

Leave. Let them destroy
Among themselves.

Remember, robots will
Pass- blow out . . . leaving
Only a stale puff of
Smoke.

Feeling/ Thought
     Never dies.

The heart beat of life.
Love itself.
Come. . . . . .
Create images that are
Real/ Beautiful.
Find your ever-lasting
     Selves.

Growing Clean

When I was a kid
I used to get up
Every saturday
Morning and wash.
Sometimes for two
Or three hours.

When I came out
I'd look at my skin
And it was so clear
I'd go to mama and say:

"Look, I'm getting white."

She'd smile, agree
And go on with her chores.
Things have changed so
Much since then.

I hardly wash any more.

Making It, or Black Corruption

Once upon a time, in truth, not very long ago, three weeks
to be exact, I use to write like Keats. I sat in my room on
the corner of Lenox and 135th and got real high on birds,
trees, animals. My whole life was aesthetics. I use to think
I was a floating ball of space.

Three weeks ago I met some very hip people. They told me
it was wrong to write of nature. They told me I had to put

down all that esoteric bull shit and come into the heat. Of course, I protested. Vehemently shouting: "Never! Never! I must always write about who I am, what I am—which is, in essence, a tree. Preferably an oak or a maple."

This week I made my New York debut. T.V. reading "Black Poetry." Now everybody's talkin'! Every time I turn around someone's tossing my name. Almost like hotcakes! You should hear them:

"Man, that cat's somethin' else" . . . . "Mean baby, mean" . . . . . . "Worse than Leroi" . . . . "Excellent, just excellent" . . . .

Why, sometimes I'm even stopped for an autograph.

Last night I went out and purchased a whole bin of ball points. Thursday I cut my hair afro, Friday change all my girl friends black, Saturday get me a nice set of pictures and resumes, Sunday rest and Monday I am flying! Wowwwwwwwww.

Yep, I am becoming quite a celebrity. Hey, maybe they'll let me have my own t.v. show? Something like "GET IT OFF YOUR CHEST" or "PENT UP EMOTION." Or perhaps they'll let me have my own variety spot? The black, Ed Sullivan.

Well, things are really going great and each morning I rise and think of all those people who taught me what it means to be

"Black And Beautiful."

R. ERNEST HOLMES

Black Lady in an Afro Hairdo
Cheers for Cassius

Honey-hued beauty, you are;
in your gleaming white shorts,
gladiator shoes,
sparkling robe of satin cream,
bursting through the ropes,
piercing the arena smoke
with your confident eyes
of Kentucky brown.
Only *now* do I realize
what it must have been like
to have known Sweet Sugar
when he was King,
or to have prayed for Joe
when the ear of the ghetto
was pressed hard
to the sound machine.
But what you bring
to the ring, no
black champ has
ever brought before—
Sweet Cassius,
you are *my* pride
in these times of pain;
fast moving,

grooving in the ring
with that pepped-up cat
who acts so bold.
Child, your hands so fast
you make the young seem old!
So, mock him once or twice
for me, baby.
Sting him 'side the head,
spin, cool Daddy,
to the side.
Ease up a bit now
and let the man ride.
Now, in the eye—
jab, jab,
Ali Shuffle,
Ooh, heavens!!
The dude is down—
Did you see it?

Black Woman

There is no mystery,
nothing secret about your movement,
Black woman.
You walk like palm trees
bending low to a beach breeze,
your hips,
see-sawing to imagined drums
and tambourines.

And I watch you
dancing
in the shadow lights,
breasts commanding the silouhettes,
fighting through the throb-beat
of soul,
your Afro hairdo hanging on
for dear life.
Shake it
shake it shake it BABY.
In steel-tipped heels on the Avenue,
100 meters with a silver baton,
Bossa Nova on the edge of sheets.
Like Brazil,
you burst in sunlight,
go mellow at dusk;
and my eyes
are your festival.

Two From the Country

I

Blacker than night
Noxema Queen,
hugh jungle-butt
in your tight blue jeans;
You dazzle 'em, baby,
with your made-up eyes,

your lavender hair
and your danger zone thighs.
Chile, do the thing
on the streets at noon,
advertise it, honey
to that shing-a-ling tune—
You'll get that boy
with the surf-blown hair,
entice him, sweets,
invite him, sweets,
to your sheets—
Black Queen.

II

Who is that gal with the syncopated hips,
the gleam in her eyes
and those foxy-looking lips?
Man, I'd like to rap to her concerning my ploy
and tell her that she's found herself
a real nature-boy.
Ooh, she's got some buns,
and her breasts are riding high.
I wonder how much sheeting-time
a Lincoln bill can buy?
Well, no time to waste,
I'll cop a taste—
at my place!
Nature-boy.

ALICIA L. JOHNSON

Monologue

El-Hajj Malik El Shabazz
                    allow me to introduce—
                                        Alicia.
(I)
        so badly want to talk to you
                                alive.
(I)
        tried to get close to you,
                            I pushed and shoved—
                                    and then heard two shots.
but then (I) knew something
                        had come between us.
you under M
                and (I)
                    under
                        A—who then shall come between us.
would you have come to see OUR WALL
                            of RESPECT
                                    when you finished speaking.
on the twenty-first of FEBRUARY?
                    you would have heard your poets praise you.
(I)
        so terribly want to
                        see you and talk to you
                                            alive.

if (I) could only meet you
                    somewhere
                    for a while/to talk
                              about your mission to MECCA
its cold here
              the snow is pinching the POET'S toes
but that's ok
    my fingers get warm when (I) touch your ice-covered
                                              statue.

won't you say a few words
                    about
                          the
                              OAAU
                                  or about
                                      my poetry:
you were a poet
              did anyone ever tell you that?
                              you spoke in prose
several times—(I) suppose—
                    nothing shall come between us
                              you under M
                                      and (I)
                    under
                        A
I shall die soon
              and be dumb
o I know we must carry on
                    but sometimes
                          dear (I) get
                              sad when others
                                    disrespect

our presence.
               would you have liked
                        the marker
                                 beneath your tomb?
it read:
       "a Prince,
               our own Black Shining Prince
               who didn't hesitate to die,
               because he loved us so."
yes
    time ends, for us all
               but somehow I doubt if
                        time really ends.
its cold
       I'm frostbitten, but
                I shall never leave until
                      I can talk to you
                          alive,
until I can recite a few poems
               before you.
(I) shall die soon
           too
           not a PRINCESS though.
                  I don't believe in them.
would you have listened
          to my poetry
              when you were hustling in harlem—
I think so—
      know—
          it was painful
              the truth
                like birth is a kind of

hurting process,
but nevertheless,
                    I could have soothed you with a poem
                    I could have rubbed your back & healed
                    your wound with/poetic stanzas.
(I)
        must leave now—
                        I so badly want to talk to you
                                                    alive
                                                    but
perhaps though
                when (I)
                        die
                        we will meet
                                    you under M
                                            and I
                                                under
                                                    A.

CHARLES JOHNSON

crossed legs

the drag of cans thrown around my mind
this a sign of time: loneliness,
tears of pain drain down my abstract face
to look upon walls of solitude,
layered stacks of love sags into one another;
for who is there to be loved

crystal clear sand beaches upon the route of escape
draining sanity from my plane . . . the black head as good
as dead.
sweet smiling pictures, separate from the flesh, that the
skin of pain . . . the kitchen drain

upon the table top below the floor she bounced from life,
guided by the text. rocking in unit segments, they tripped
beyond my feet.
i sat as many times before, alone in solitude, to watch the
perpetual roll of the waves . . . i'm a slave it can be.

lightly painted daughters of middle class faces drive stakes
of dead illusions into my spine . . . board stiff the waves
showed no riff.

bound by dimensions of physically established unit
components to drift.
birds releasing clouds of deviation, a half fad of make
believe students, attempt their acknowledgement.

those not aware of socialization, only engulfed in it,
in prevailing un-uniform conformity among those of
anarchy.
shiftless individuals seeking concrete feet, to walk the stone
path of secondary group inter-action.
daughters of economic slaughter puff lightly upon 10-cent
love norms.

the surreal world of the functionalized, organized brave-
land.
home of forgotten children locked in the outer-room,
the hawk murdering in-effectionate, senile killer of
black people, of black people, of black people, of brown
people,

of brown people, of brown people, of red people, of red
people,

of red people, of yellow people, of yellow people, of
yellow people. . . . dead,

they all dead

the parking lot world of sergeant pepper

a room full of bones.
frozen plates of lemonade, empty of feeling, controlled by
    small psychotic men of gin . . .
the feet of birds, dipped in easter eggs, I looked out, the
    plastic flask of my molded mask . . .

sticked woman of hate, in Kellogg's corn flakes, as once gas
     head chubby checker did shake,
          the punk's a fake . . .

pink shoes, fan blues . . . Praise the lord, and pay you dues,
incidentally, use birth control pills cause the lord ain't the
     only one who screws.

extremist of conventional, same as stereotype, almost,
     would if I could, be, . . . people
          jesus christ farted; the construction of civilization
               an amoeba squeaked . . . eight ball in the corner pete.

1, 2, 3, demons breakfast of grapes and swine, and shit face
     script writers who make
          T.V. bore . . . and they never fucked a whore . . .
Mantu—— . . . or shall we say split plains of destruction,
     did you force you child and
he rebelled . . . and died, and went to hell . . .
     "thank you," saided the little pink train, as old age
     flush him down the drain.

Isolation defined; a man's bleached dry skull, frozen in gum
     wrappers and placed on a
floating plane, within his predetermined slot, then left to
     rot, with his eyes wide open . . .
sweet dance of natives on the fore-ground of the liquor
     store, they all desire the door,
not to be poor.
End definition: psyche in stereo piped chaos, such as dish
     pan hands, skilled wounds,
snotty nose *toddlers*, and blistered feet . . .

"I" . . . figure that out punks (dull normals and
morons also included)
Brass feet of elephant teeth, hidden under the table cloth,
beneath floor above the
trap door . . . did Moses snore?
The glass knife of loneliness, fore the suit of wool, to cut
the flesh of man, Sgt.
Pepper didn't play in no bands . . . the secret man, with
process grease and gas in his
hands . . . and black folk ran the South, and ran them, a
nude man brung in an edition of
"life" . . . dead, castrated. I'm black and dirty but guilt is
filth.

Soft tones or cars crashing, in the midst of _____ frog
intestines . . . the '56 haug
(trade name: Buick Special '56) pulled to the corner and
dropped . . . low (referring to
hydraulic lifts). The ark of Noah wrapped in Sgt. Pepper's
gas (which is the ghetto),
still undiscovered.

HERSCHELL JOHNSON

To Mareta

I miss you now
as always
and as always
I know
that the time
spent with you
is not time enough
and that
there can
never be TIME/enough

remembrances of early mornings
of waking still hugged from the night before
and you are asleep
and I am lonely.

that is perhaps selfish.

I know.
but I want every moment to be our moment
every dream our dream
every breath our life
every touch without separation.

for love
you are just that
and it is you
that completes me

I think of afternoons
and it is autumn
              or perhaps spring
and even if it is winter
              it is yet summer
because all thoughts
         of afternoons
              are thoughts of you
and all thoughts of you

are warm thoughts
         yes love
     they are
         warm thoughts

it is nightfall
         and the stars have yet to make their appearance

but the moon is out/ALREADY

yes love

         the darkness is you just as the light is
         just as summer winter fall spring all are

you

         and I think
         and you are
         and I dream
         and it is your fantasy

MARETA

              your name
              a fantasy as real as touch

as true as I love you
mareta/FOR
you are my life
as the sun's glow
is the tree's green

as you/me/I/you/we are US

experiencing the experience
of being
of knowing the importance/TO BE

TOGETHER

"We Are Not Mantan"

WE ARE NOT MANTAN
or BUCK/wheat

false comic images
singers&dancers
a heritage

is not what is made
like T.V.'s
but what is

we are
HANNIBAL
coming through the alps
and SHAKA
defending his homeland

and NAT TURNER
spreading black terror
through the fields

        we are
        those who were
        warriors
        and who entertained
        the man with death.

ALICE H. JONES

For Sapphire, My Sister

Woman with hoe in hand, and baby on your back,
Sorrow-sated and tired to apathy,
My sister:

I oil your skin, manicure your feet, take hookworm from your
Children,
Your man takes back his spear.

I turn your sweat into perfume and your breasts into onyx-
tipped
Fruit.
I erase the erosions of childbearing from your stomach
And the robbers of your teeth have replaced them with
pearls
And the scent of honeysuckle.
I give desire again, when your man comes
And if immortality slips, screaming, from your loins,
I give you joy to replace despair.

The river gives its many-tongued kisses as you bathe;
It does not hide the crucified body of your brother.
The rope holds clothes and draws water from the well;
It does not hold the dead and blackened fruit, that once
was
Your neighbor.
The fire warms your home and the bones of your old:

It does not roast your screaming son under the sign of
    Jesus.

I give you handmaidens, not a boss lady;
Bodyguards, not the Klan.
I give you a castle, with peacocks in the garden:
You will never know of shacks with flies or tenements with
    rats.
I give you incense, hummingbird tongues in honey,
Sandals of beaten gold and bracelets of ivory.

I give you jewels and crowns for your velurial hair
And rings for your ebony hands.
I give you the Kings of Benin at your feet
And lands to the rim of the world.

Woman with hoe in hand, and baby on your back,
Sorrow-sated and tired to apathy,
My sister:
I oil your skin, manicure your feet, take hookworm from
    your
Children,
Your man takes back his spear.

ARNOLD KEMP

A Black Cop's Communion

RIOT! screamed the studs
   and cleared the streets of all
      but night
    flitting rats that swim the jungle
      sewers and live on sour
        baby's breath

RIOT! man I loaded
   my pistol and ran screaming
      gone wild
   in the heat of a hot gun's roar
     slaying a boy in the mirror
      named Juan

    Such a Harlem waste
     while
    Alabama soil
  lies virgin and fertile
  in the Easter glow

Guilt Redeemed

If Nero lived today
               he could wander
the streets of Harlem
               fiddling the flames
and blame the Christians
        Rightly

How to Succeed
(*For niggers only*)

Don't fight Boy!
         That's not the American
                    Way!
Laugh, sing, dance,
        Grin, hope and
                  Pray.

Hello Blackness
(*Inspired by a poem by Guyon Cain*)

Hello Blackness
Can I talk to you?
Beautiful, bursting, burning Blackness
Black as coal
Black as the depths of
The unknown heavens

Don't turn away
Can I talk to you?
Can I tell you of all the proud black dreams
Of a warrior's heart?
Can I enter the you that is me and become
Flesh of your flesh

Hello Brown
Can I talk to you?
Pretty, pleasing, pulsating brown
Brown as earth
Brown as the warm colors of love
Don't turn your head
Can I talk to you?
Can I plant in you the seed
Of tomorrow's black world?
Can I paint the face of your beauty
Upon the faces of my sons?

Hello Tan
Can I talk to you?
Teasing, taunting, tantilizing Tan
Tan as fresh wood
Tan as sun-tinted African fruit
Don't turn me off
Can I talk to you?
Can I fill you with all
The manhood that is Me?
Can we together bring
The wrath of Black Gods
Down upon this dying earth?

Hello yellow
Can I talk to you?
Yellow, yellow, mellow yellow
Yellow as sun beams
Yellow as the golden hope
Of our tomorrow day
Don't be sad
You're mine too
Can I talk to you?
Can I tell you of all the lies
That have kept us apart?
Lies that have kept us from building
Our multi-colored kingdom
Over this globe of white tyranny.
Can I tell you of rape?
Can I tell you of hunger
And of beatings
And of freckle-faced house niggers
Crawling to the master's bedroom
Oh yellow, yellow, mellow yellow
You've been running with the wrong people
For such a long time
Welcome back home baby
Hello brown, tan, cocoa, beige, chocolate,
Coffee, gold, bronze, yellow, ebony
Hello Blackness
Hello Blackness
Can I talk to you?

The End of the World

It's the end of the world!
It's the end of the world!
It's the end of the world!
It's the end of the white world!
It's the end of the white world!
All over the world white idols are crumbling
upon their pedestals of evil
All over the world white temples are sinking
into the mud of their own iniquities
It's the end of the world!
It's the end of the world!
It's the end of the world!
It's the end of the white world!
It's the end of the white world
Cause
Black people ain't crying no more
Black people ain't praying no more
Black people ain't begging no more
Black people have declared war
No talk of mercy, no thought of peace,
No cries of innocence
All are guilty by birth
The sons of rapists must pay
For their fathers' orgasms.
Fire erupts from every window
Blond bodies float in the air like white ash
Blue-eyed babies cry hungrily
Over dead mothers with no breasts
It's the end of the world!
It's the end of the world!

It's the end of the world!
It's the end of the white world!
It's the end of the white world
Cause
Black people ain't praying no more
Black people ain't crying no more
Black people ain't begging no more
Black people have gone to war

A thick cloud hangs over every city
Brothers have all rebelled
Police are killing police
Soldiers are deserting their battlefields
Terror is the order of the day
Death whistles through the night with a scream
Deep, deep within the subterranean bowels of the earth
Honkie devils fight to push the button
That will destroy their own mothers
Push the button Honkie!
Push the button Honkie!
Push the button Honkie!
Kill us all Honkie!
Kill us all Honkie
Cause
Black people ain't crying no more
Black people ain't praying no more
Black people ain't begging no more
Black people have gone to war

It is now a half century later
The smoke has finally cleared the horizon
Peace has at last come to all the world

People now wear white to mourn and black to celebrate
Metamorphosis has swept the earth
Even cotton now grows black
Little children sit and listen
To the tales the old folk tell
They tell of the day the white man went insane
And tried to blow up the whole world
They tell of the millions of whites who died
From skin radiation.
Laughingly, they tell of the Blacks who lived
Protected by skin pigmentation.
And there, there in the clean pure air of that
Free day my son's son walks proudly
Without shame or fear
His eyes are sparkling with a warrior's pride
His heart bursting with the glory of his
Grandfather's courage.
Like a king he walks down
Huey Newton street,
Crosses over to
Muhammed Ali square,
Enters a house on
Eldridge Place,
In the county of
Martin Luther King,
In the city of
Marcus Garvey,
In the state of
Malcolm
And all this came to be
Cause

Black people ain't crying no more
Black people ain't praying no more
Black people ain't begging no more
At last
Black people have gone to war.

Love Me Black Woman

Love me Black Woman
Love me with the love
We lost on the hulking
Ships of slave merchants
Love me with the strength
Of the clanking chains
That tore flesh from
Our bone
Love me with all the
Black blood that watered
Fields of nations
Built upon our backs
Love me Black Woman
Love me
Love me with the hot rhythms
of our ancestral drums
The eternal fires of
Sacred black altars
Love me with the warm press
Of your thighs

And the soft swell of your belly
Filled with the children of our union
Love me Black Woman
Woman, woman, Oh Black Woman
Mother of the universe
Breeder of a million kings
Woman, Oh Black Woman
You who crawled with me
When I could not stand
Stood with me
When I could not walk
Lay with me
When I was unworthy
Woman, Oh Black Woman
Mother of all the shades
Of the rainbow
Love me, love me
Love me Black Woman
Love me now that I am worthy
Love me now that I am Man
Love me with the love that
Made me Man
The love that will make me a giant
The love that can make me a god
Love me Black Woman
Love me
Love me
Love me

LEYLAND KING

"I could never ask you"

I could never ask you
. . . to stay . . . So,
When you drift away
Be the same you to me.
For, you are the
Limit of yourself in
being what you are.
And you are the
Nicest
Fun and Fantasy
combination of
Playful seriousness.
(and I love you)
I'll sing my mind to rest
with your memory
and wish your reality
the best
of the best
(Wondering if the time
will ever come
when something
I will never use
will be thrown out
of a dormant state
into . . .

Subdued patterns of life
and living . . .)
Stroke each strand of hair
for me
whisper your name at six and six
And if you ever need me
just stop . . .
and so will I
Take care of Aki
(how I envy her)
    Thank-you
for the beads, and buttons
and your smile.
And I trust the times
will change
    to reveal
what I dare not conjecture
    But if I did . . . no,
I could never ask you
. . . to stay . . . So,
When you drift away
Be the same you to me.
For you are the
Limit of yourself in
being what you are.
And you are the
Nicest
Fun and Fantasy
combination of
Playful seriousness.
(and I love you)

"Didn't it come like a tidal wave"

Didn't it come like
    a tidal wave.
    Booming, crashing,
carrying a ton of sand
    for your eyes,
uncaring?
                Oh, but it did.
No eyes to see
distractions of other
obstacles,
    . . . then it lost incentive,
        and not—and . . . so—
and lost inertia and time
    in the shuffle,
and like a helpless tear
            surrendered
to create the sea it was
        before.
If it ever comes again
        run into it.
It's me.

JEWEL C. LATIMORE
(Johari Amini)

Masque

a sister false is
cause
to make one bleed

it makes one wonder
how and why
as black becomes
as white
and smiles and is the same
and seems the same
and seemingly the blackness
has not changed . . .

and yet we are betrayed

Utopia

brothers
brothers
everywhere—
and
not a one
for Sale.

DON L. LEE

Re-Act for Action
(*For brother H. Rap Brown*)

re-act to animals:
> cage them in zoos.

re-act to inhumanism:
> make them human

re-act to nigger toms:
> with spiritual acts of love & forgiveness
> or with real acts of force.

re-act to yr/self:
> or are u too busy tryen to be cool
> like tony curtis & twiggy?

re-act to whi-te actors:
> understand their actions;
> faggot actions & actions against yr/dreams

re-act to yr/brothers & sisters:
> love.

re-act to whi-te actions:
> with real acts of blk/action.
> BAM BAM BAM

re-act to act against actors
who act out pig-actions against
your acts & actions that keep
you re-acting against their act & actions
stop.
act in a way that will cause them

to act the way you want them to act
in accordance with yr/ acts & actions:
              human acts for human beings
re-act
NOW niggers
& you won't have to
act
false-actions
at
your/children's graves.

In the Interest of Black Salvation

Whom can I confess to?
The Catholics have some cat
They call father,
              mine cutout a long time ago—
Like His did.
I tried confessing to my girl,
But she is not fast enough—except on hair styles,
                        clothes
                        face care and
                        television.
If ABC, CBS, and NBC were to become educational
    stations
She would probably lose her cool,
                    and learn to read
Comic Books.

My neighbor, 36-19-35 volunteered to listen but
I couldn't talk—
Her numbers kept getting in the way,
Choking me.
To a Buddhist friend I went,
Listened, he didn't—
Advise, he did,
        "pray, pray, pray and keep one eye open."
I didn't pray—kept both eyes open.

Visited three comrades at Fort Hood,
There are no Cassandra cries here,
No one would hear you anyway. They didn't.
Three tried to speak, "don't want to make war."
                                    why???
When you could do countless other things like
Make life, this would be—
Useless too . . .

When I was 17,
I didn't have time to dream,
Dreams didn't exist—
Prayers did, as dreams.
I am now 17 & 8,
I still don't dream.
Father forgive us for we know what we do.
Jesus saves,
            Jesus saves,
                    Jesus saves—S & H Green Stamps.

TENA L. LOCKETT

The Almost Revolutionist

One black brother with good intentions
and nappy hair and brown sandals
and a cloth sack of black books
which added weight to a heavy gun
on his half-healed shoulder of his arm of his hand
which he used to use
to smooth his natural
when times got hot and hair got kinky
at brutal battles
at conference tables
in days of old.
          SO
One black brother with good intentions
and nappy hair and brown sandals
took 3 seconds to shift the weight
to raise the hand
to smooth the natural
to square the shoulders
while whitey saw him
and slew him
as in the days of old.

JAMES R. LUCAS

The Beat

This is about the size of it, Dad.
Time just hasn't done, for me, the things
You said it would.
It's been a bad scene all the way 'round.
Like you told me to play it cool—wait for the happenings.
And I said, "Yeah."
So I just dug the sounds.
Old *Life* rolled squeaking out of Prez's horn
And Lady Day came on.
Yardbird squealed the hurt and I dug it all.
And cooled it.
But those cats were just like me, Dad.
They weren't moving.
Not really into anything.
They knew the bad deal and spat it out on wax.
But they weren't going anyplace.
Somehow I've had it, Baby; up to here.
The main sounds, now, come floating out of Malcolm's ax—
Stokely and Rap sit in as side men.
And little shriveled-up Jimmy Baldwin's phrase
Is telling it like it is: "God gave Noah the Rainbow sign.
                              No more water—the fire next time."
I got to get with it, Dad.
I got to *make* it—on *this* set . . .

BOB MAXEY

Moses Miles

When the good woman who raised me
some 70 plus years ago
got ready to release life, she said:
"Moses, take your lantern
and meet me down hard by the big rock.
I may be a little late, but you wait for me
hard down by the big rock."

Well sur, she never made it so I buried her
near the pine tree next to her good husband, Will.

Now that I've cheated the good lord
out of 70 or 80 years
and He wants to collect his debts from me
I feel like I'm about ready to go—
except for one thing. Just one thing.

If I could just make the folks around here
call me by my rightful name!
Sometimes I feel like sayin to em,
"Call me Moses. Moses Miles.
Don't croon my name lik you talkin to a cryin' baby
or soft woman. Don't say 'moz,' or 'mo,' or 'mooze.'
Give my name a full sound,
Like you would when talking about the first
one that had that name.

Say, "MOHZESS MILES." Full, big and rich.
Say, "MOHZESS MILES."

All my life that's been my biggest battle.
If I had been summoned, condemned or cursed
in sounds that sounded like: MOHZESS MILES
IS A BASE CUR! MOHZESS MILES IS A DANGEROUS
MAN! MOHZESS MILES IS A UPPITY NIGGER!
I would have known by the very way they called
my name that I would have already won.
But folks around here never called my name
with a serious sound to it.

Well now, after 70 or 80 years it becomes
a less troublesome notion for me.
As it turned out my life wasn't half bad.
Maybe that's because a good woman raised me.
She always taught me that I was to talk to every man
in a clear tone; look him straight in the eye;
never bow my head lower than his hairline;
learn to count as high as the money you'll git;
learn that the easiest thing to do is cheat a man
out of his woman, money and pride, so don't do none
of that. Because it's too cosy; get along with drunks,
preachers, and women of the night, and above all, never
but never lose fear but never fear what you got to do.

Well, I learned most them things and as it turned out
my life wasn't half too bad at that.
Had two fights in my life—one time came close to
be'in killed, other came close to killin.
But I learned from both them times.

Been able to do some travelin in my time. Worked every
corner of this country. Worked every sort of job.
Railroading, section nine gang, loggering, deckhanding,
farming, mining, cooking, cleaning, even worked
one time out west as a watcher. (That's a feller
hired by the gambling hall to watch the dealer—I ofen
wonder who they had to watch me!) One job
I had I was a baggage-handler and general whatnot
for a travellin minstrel show—and some show that was too!
So you can see, I seen sometin of the world.

But I finally came back here to this place to settle.
Most my life been spent right here. Been able to
wrestle a bigger piece of land from em through the
years, and it's worked out fairly well. I suppose
I came back here because this is where my roots are.
Might sound strange cause mos white folks around here
don't call my name in respectful ways, but I always felt
stronger and more rooted here than anyplace else.
If a white man up north call me "sur" didn't mean
half as much as if white folks around here in this
county would call me Mohzess Miles.
Guess that's why I came back here.

Guess it was for the best that I never took a wife
nor had no children. Way things are around here
and the way I am I guess my love for a woman would
have turned sour after a while and my pride in my
children would have turned cold. Did meet one woman
I could have married one time, though.
Now there was a prize beauty! She was a virtuous woman
finely built wid blazin eyes, high chin and a color

like the very fires of hell. Her color was like a blood red
injun summer sun coolin under her soft black skin.
There was a woman! She had a way of lookin at a man
which would say: now, I know you want me, but do you
have what it takes to git me.

Well, Lord knows I tried to take her. I really tried to
take her. But she finally went to another gent.
Fellow from up north, upstanding with fine principles
and a good mind. They married and I came to learn
he got killed in some kind of disturbance up in Detroit.
Civil Rights or some such damn thing. Last I heard of
her she was a broken woman praying for death to take her.
She died soon after softly callin that gentleman's name.
I guess I wasn't man enough to have her cause it seems
every bit of her soul was spent on that fine gentleman
who won her.

Been feelin a bit poorly lately s'pose its bout my
time to go. But one thing is real funny. Now that I
am about ready to die I never had so many visitors from
the white folks around here in my life. Want "to buy . . .
my land. They say its for a 'big industrial park'
say, i'm holdin back progress for my people if I don't
sell to them. Say I'm stoppin the upliftin of my people
if I don't sell these here 400 acres to em.

Well sur, I'll never sell. No Sir, I'll never sell!
I'm dyin' now, so let them courts and lawyers
settle it after I die.
But I'll never sell to em.
Not until they all start callin me
MOHZESS MILES!!

blues

it will all get explained
one day, it will all get written down
i mean, the story of blues.
what other theme means a damn?
except, that one.
i'm talkin' about:

> moody
> sooty
> pitiless
> pitless
> deepintheguts
> lawforming
> heavysetting
> disintergrating
> malfunctioning
> world-swallowing
> blues-triggering
> misbegotton
> unforgiving
> three-o'clock-in-the-
> morning
> kind of blues

one day it will all get explained
sooner or later
it is bound to get put down on paper
with a best way to be said
kind of style.
In poem, song or cry
by poet, singer or mournful griever

the message must get explained
about a:

> head-rolling
> finger-popping
> toe-tapping
> blues-singing
> I'm too-wise-for-the-world
> if-i-had-my-life-to-live-over
> i'm born a jew kind of blue

it's hard to explain the message of blues
to smooth-seeking folks.
because blues-knowing folks don't believe in
none of that smoothing-out kind of action.

no man! blues-ridden folks don't believe in
none of that smoothing-out kind of action.
no man! blues-ridden folks don't need none of that!
because they've grabbed from:

> galloping ghosts
> street tamers
> prudish whores
> uptight bankers
> simple-assed farmers
> smiling-eyed
> campus cuties

the message of blues from A to Z.

where do you go to find out about blues?
where do you find out about the blackness of blues?

sailors sing blues while drifting
on dazzling bright oceans
comedians can cause chortles and chuckles
though gripped by the blues
northern tundras capped with whiteness
can tell about the blackness of blues.
more southern climes, brillant with
white sands can tell about the blackness
of blues.

waiters on paydays
truck drivers on payless days
prelates, prime ministers
professors, pundits
have been known to cohabitate
with blues.

who knows about that remarkable
affliction called blues?

the baby knows it
the drunk senses it
the dying lover sees it
the righteous fears it
the father feels it

Who concedes to that godawful
asleep-in-the-deep kind of blues?

the pundit shuns it
the sinner taunts it
the mother ignores it
the lonely ones smile at it
the activists run from it

Who among you never knew
that kind of blue?

the proud ones sidestep it
the whore lives it
the preacher smothers it
the giant begs of it
the nothings bore of it

Baby believe! it's a genuine man's
malaise to fancy up and call:

weltschmerz
soulsick
jaded
jaundiced
blasé

but baby, it's all the same
it's a:

goodbad
hurtpleasant
sad, sad, knowing
you got to be sad
kind of thing.

some day it will all get explained.
about the:

disconnected
disjointed
lowlifting
downswinging

gut-splitting
heart-skipping
that's-how-it-is
that's-what-it-is
that's-how-it's-got-to-be
kind of thing.

The City Enscriber

1. The Poet of Urban Affairs
   whose task it is
   to mark the spot of our transgressions
   and perhaps point to a solution
   finds his job impossible.
   No witty rhymes or gentle passages
   can guide his pen, nor can he find
   puissant prose to sway and titilate
   the bleeding streets.
   He has no pristine talent
   to manufacture a Muse
   that would move his uncaring audience.
   The Poet of Urban Affairs
   pulls upon his head the virus
   of art disgraced as he tries to
   sing about the shipwreck of the builders' dream—
   the bleeding, condemned city.
   The Urban Poet
   finds nothing to sing to
   in the cold concrete.

He can evoke no emotion in the
coldly pulling and tussling mob.
There is nothing standing on street corners
to make him recall moments of calm reflection.
Can he ode an elergy to what dies in tenements?
What happens on the roof, in the subway,
on the block, that can compel him to
capture and preserve with his inscriptions?
The City Poet,
Bard of the Megalopolis,
is building his art on promises of tomorrow
and he is not able to capture the cold slabs
of indifference to heed his utterances.

2. Hey Poet!
   Who's out there to listen to you!
   Nothing but CityFolk.
   Cold and trembling people
   caring not one wit for your
   music and meter.
   Impotent grandfathers glancing towards you
   when the scene gets less hurtful elsewhere.
   Old babies and infant elders
   recalling to themselves forgotten promises.
   A bent-backed people whiffing glorious dreams
   while stuck on the stiffling, stenched-stoops
   where CityFolk sit.

3. Poet of Urban Affairs,
   when will you wake up!
   If you intend to have the laureate
   of CityFolk

you should let your writing hand
paint plans of their long-denied paradise
while your fighting hand demand's the things
that are theirs.
Write of "doom"; "soon"
cast away "june"; "moon"
Write as their correspondent of war
and stand behind rooftop barricades
and when time permits, write this:

Blood now heat city concrete.
Dreams of the Nation must be delivered.
Black Daughters are birthing illegimate Warriors.
Black Mothers play fools for eight dollars a day.
Black Fathers bow and smile to subvert the enemy.
Black Sons snipe devils from rat-infested bunkers.
Black Death is being ordained by a CityFolk—
Now Just Born.

4. Hey Dillatante Poet!
What mission keeps you from
sensing their plight?
What sublime images rob you of a sight
of the sources of their dangerous feats?
What Muses do you now honor
from other times and places
that stills the pace of your singing pen?
What tradition of art
holds you from painting the faces
of the faceless CityFolk?
You may think that your romantic gaze
of the city scene

can mask the writhing mass
of the CityFolk.
But it will not!
The desperate cares of CityFolk,
The dark lairs of CityFolk,
will trap you someday
you damn CityPoet!

DON A. MIZELL

"I Want You To Hear Me"

I WANT YOU TO HEAR ME. as a volcano screeching and
    sprung to the sea, connecting & burning all it must
    touch,
you are that to me.
i could show you these tears i've baked and plea.
nippled, pungent
    desperately. For good reason, i would think:
        if those rivers had swollen, run swollen to the
        earth, run
like flowed fingers too early in the morning. or spring's
grateful burst quenching the thirst of death/gone singeing
to the sea; if they would only hear me girl
    i want to tell you want you
now that reasons abound and i can smell again
    you know
speak of life again
    and mean it.

    or scream it quite secretly let me *tell* you woman:
explosions are occurring in colored town and if you listen
you will hear your father too. Hungry.
    Fleece me sister
fleece me all night long
say:Hey
    yeah,

you in the jungle
wit yo panties traced
          um yo niggah.
you know?

"Hope was faced alone":

Hope was faced alone:
Quietly and desperately
And perfectly.
Never touching: never reaching
          out to be touched.

This life surprises, tho';
Keeps bringing those miracles
Right up in your goddamn face
And pukking joy all over you.

It was cold here
And it was getting colder
The ice had settled long ago,
Smothering a warm belly.

                    So when the fire descended
                    When the fire came up
                    I was completely freaked:
                    A whole new thing.

Let me say it: Time must wait
Let me say it: I think you got me by the nuts.
          And I really don't mind.

A. X. NICHOLAS

This Baptism with Fire . . .

The shouts shrink to a tense
silence. Trembling tongues
of fire turn to ashes.
The invisible blood burning
in our black faces—we huddle
bitterly at bay in this hovel—
cops clutching their stiff
rifles—eager to kill.

This baptism with fire, people,
is our redemption—our kindled candle.
Our dreams have long ago drowned
in the guts of the sea. We leap
blindly at dragons—our bloody bones
bolting through the skin's edge.

(For Lee)

Let me   Blackpeople   Let me
touch your ears/
leave a history-of-ourselves
in words/in songs/
some sign
that we live/that we die
in search-of-warmth/in search-of-worth in this world.
Where . . . wheres there a liberated land
in which to move/to direct our dreams?
We're exiled within America/
& the shadow-of-Blackwomen
raped by the oppressor's lust
stagger in our doses-of-sleep.
I say
we're exiled within America/
& the shadows-of-Blackmen
poking fantasties into their veins
stagger in our doses-of-sleep/
& long lights of cop-cars spill over-into the streets
into hated shapes over the walls of the ghetto/
& we hurl bloody fire into their faces as
loud proof-of-revolution on the march!

(For Mack)

A net-of-smoke
hovers over this bar/
& Im stuck here

with my drowned dreams.
                    Who am I/Who am I
breathing whiskey in this mirror?
                    Who am I/Who am I
with this rage
              that wont move
beyond a mouth-of-words?
                    To learn how to live with
the deceptions-of-myself *is* my failed manhood.
                        Where/Wheres the bravery
in my blood/
                not the posture-of-adventurists
that defies the grave/
                but the as-simple-as act of defining myself
in the image I choose as a Black man.
                        The story is as-long-as
4 centuries: why I wait here for some whore/
the naked craving
                to touch/to feel live flesh/
the naked craving
                to tell/to convince myself
that Im a man in a world carved in dead ice.
                                Theres
the dead certainty of all departures: a train
trails off/
              the snow & "my woman's gone now. . . ."
It's hell baby to be left lonely
like this
          Do our histories end
          at this hour?
          How lasting

are words/How far
do they reach beyond their sounds upon the tongue?
I distrust them: words we once created
as a human stance against all that is ugly in the world.
What is it
that blinds us to the beauty we share
as Black man/as Black woman?
C'mon back!
Let me wear your dark flesh warm against this cold.
Can you hear/Can you hear
this hurt?
I say
it's hell baby to be left lonely
like this/
& how long to drag my shadow
down & over all of these strange & white streets?

(For Poki)

1.

Strange
that we wake
in the center of the night/
the naked image-of-ourselves
locked black & beautifully together on this bed.

2.

The sand & miles-of-water
before us/
            our Black bodies
blending with this night/
            the far city
floating (How strange!) in this sky.

3.

Strange
            how your thighs
tremble like the tomtom-of-drums in the night/
            opening/closing
hot & dark as Africa round my waist.

RAYMOND R. PATTERSON

Invitation

Come into my black hands.
Touch me. Feel the grip
And cramp of angry circumstance
In each finger tip. Hold them
Burning to your lips. Taste
The hard
Bitter argument with God
Engendered in the skin—
The unhealed bruise
Inherited—like sin.
Tell me what you understand.

See the nails,
Where the nails are hammered in
And broken? . . . where the flesh is dead
Under the thick rust? What is to be said
That does not touch on lust?
Where will you begin
To heal my deep distrust?

These hands you made!
Across each palm, these scars,
Track upon track, were laid,
And grief passed over grief
And nothing stayed that was not black.
It is that odor of despair

You sense when my hands draw near.
What are dust or stars?

Listen!
It has come to this:
My right hand waits on an iron wrist,
Five fingers like knife blades set in a trap.
My left hand sways in the air, its palm cupped.
Come closer. Hear the left hand clap.

ARTHUR PFISTER

The Poet's Guilt

that man
            there
    reading from
                    rotted   sweated
                        pages
that man
        there
            crystallizing
                his/our
            drab
                existences
        to the   eyes
                of
                    his   audiences
            "what's the muthafucka doing"
            "why's the muthafucka talking
                                talking"
                    when
                            bullets
                whir
                    and   pigs
                            feast
                        on   those   people   like
                            that   man
                                        there

If She Bees

*(A poem written while loving my
grandmother's eyes; the eyes of her . . . words)*

what
     will make
          me think
               she bees
                    . . . soulful
          or
               t'gthr
          or
               her walk
                    . . . a poem
               swishing & slashing
               —breathstopping—
her smile
her lips
          the mother of my eyes
          the father of my realself
          the MADDEST, BADDEST sister
                    . . . of my dreams
her words
          singing rampant melodies
          of
               highways
                    boxcars
                         & niggers . . .
what
     will make
          me think
               she bees
                    —mine—

will she come
        as
            i would come
                 (spouting poems?)
or
  will she come
            eyes creamed
                . . . tearful
will
    she come
          a greek in her soul
             or
               magnifying our/herself
                  a living
                    breathing image
                      of the motherland . . .
or will
    she come
      with her Blackness
            well/combed
               shining
                 . . . upon her head
      owning
         almost everything
            . . . but her mind
will
    something
         make-her/move-her/groove-her/
         take-her/maker
            as faker

          & take-me/make-me
            ... sing the blues?
yeah,
    brother
        i believe in the blues ...
        i believe in
            the blues ...
        I BELIEVE IN THE BLUES!!!
            I DO!!!
                i do
                    i do
                        (brother)

but
    love ain't blue
        ... it's *Black*
      if
        she comes
            blue
              ... she knows the exit
                'cause poems aren't written
                  ... to quell a woman
                    (not *Black* poems)
but
    if she comes
    if she bees
          if she bees
            if she bees
              if she bees
                IF SHE BEES!!!
                  ... *Black*

          she'll know
          she'll know
                (& her momma will, too)

If Beer Cans Were Bullets

and our
    namby-nimby-pamby-pimby shuffles
        were
            REAL ma-a-a-a-a-annnn
    we could
        wreck their boorish party
        & turn it into their *nite*-mares
            ma-a-a-a-a-a-annnnnnnnnn
    we could make
            any/body no no/body
            & no/body no any/body
            'cause ma-a-a-a-annnnnnnnnn
            the bodilesses' bodys
        would
            over-out/body ANY no/body
            and the no/bodies
            would be the bo/dys
            the no/bodys nevuh noo
                ma-a-a-a-a-a-a-a-annnnnnnnnn
            if we could
                shave *some*
        and condemn zebra-striped craniums
                ma-a-a-a-a-a-a-a-annnnnnnnnnnnnn

and make the unreal
>   FO-REAL
>   &
dig
ma-a-a-a-a-a-a-a-a-annnnnnnnn
>   sever
filter-tipped-silver-lipped-vocab-tripped
>   "LIBERALS"
>   & lonely bro's
>   lacking sisters fingers
>   ma-a-a-a-a-annnnnnnnn
>   we COULD
>   ma-a-a-a-a-a-a-annnnnnnn
>   we could
>   ma-a-a-a-annnnn
>   if beer cans
>   was bullets
>   ma-a-a-a-a-a-a-annnnnnnnn
>   and tongues
>   . . . missiles

Ode to the Idiots

*(For all man-tanned whitee-boys who
devil-delve in OREO, cream-sandwiched,
fudge-rippled, jew-boy bags)*

they
>   *were*

                    our leaders
they . . .
    them . . .
            those . . . siss/ied/need/weed/off/keyed/weak/
                    kneed/Blackseed/needing/plead/deed
                    "please-please-please"
                            . . . pleasing
                                . . . pleading
                                    . . . bleeding
                                        . . . *niggers*!!!!!!!!
they
    were
            pray/ing-in-a-church
                            . . . and marchin'
            watch/ing-nite/sticks-lurch
                            . . . and marchin'
            pick/e/ting-large-stores
                            . . . and marchin'
            lov/ing-blue/eyed-whores
                            . . . and marchin'
            say/ing-prayers-out-loud
                            . . . and marchin'
            bee/ing-beige-and-proud
                            . . . and marchin'
            kill/ing-ow/er-minds
                            . . . and marchin'
            bust/ing-our-bee-hinds
                            . . . and marchin'
            lov/ing-kill/er-eyes
                            . . . and marchin'

lov/ing-snow/white-thighs
>... and marchin'
loo/zing-pairs-of-shoes
>... and marchin'
pay/ing-month/ly-dues
>... and marchin'
>... and marchin'
>... and marchin'
>... and marchin'
... we got/ta'
o/pen-up-our-eyes
>... and know/them
cease-their-gold/cold-lies
>... and know/them
o/pen-up-our-hearts
>... and know/them
blot-their-burn/ing-warts
>... de/stroy them
>... de/stroy them
>... de/stroy them
>... de/stroy them
... *they*
>... THEM
>... THOSE
>siss/ied/need/weed/off/keyed/weak/
>kneed/Blackseed/needing/plead/deed
>"please-please-please"
>... pleasing
>... pleading
>... bleeding
>... NIGGERS!!!!!!!!!!!!

HERBERT LEE PITTS

Reality

Natural mop
       & political rap
African
       dressed—wearin' Banlon socks
Morehouse trained
       still playin' on the "American Dream"
Following King
       while stereo-typin' "Rap's" thing
Middle class coon
       locked in "The Man's" killin' zone
Try to escape if you will
       but nigger you'll soon see
       that when "The Man" talks about
       "The Problem"
He dam' sure just don't mean me!!!!!!

We Must Lead

Brothers
Who
Will
Lead
Us?

130

They say Black Leadership
& We
Leftovers/sons & daughters
Of a wretched people
Taken
In chairs across the waters
Havin eaten of the fruits of disunity
& willin'ly paid for our own misery
There's no room for self-pity
Sorrow doesn't free us
The pitiful are unprotected and selfish
And easily denied of freedom
So many subjected this year

They say Black Leadership
& We struggle blindly
Marchin' out of our own communities
Into theirs (dig me S.C.L.C.)
Leaving our homefront unprotected
On the block, in the street
Down Fifth Avenue
In front of the U.N.
A hippie with an African dressed nigger
        holding *her* hand
Who reads Longfellow
In Washington Square
Black revolutionaries
Character assassinatin'
Black revolutionaries: leaflets/magazines/
                    newspapers/radio/t.v.
                    Speeches—"crisis"

"The Liberator," "Ramparts,"
"Newsweek," "Time," etc.

Brothers
Who
Will
Lead
Us?

Black Leadership will never
Be the new nigger
With middle class expectations
Asked me "How far in college I went"
I said "Did you dig on Fanon at Howard?"
Him still tryin' to find a reply
He
Another swahili-speakin' faggot
Wears Ivy-League dashiki
Made at Burlington Industries
From cotton grown & hand picked in Alabama
Field director for/ Local HEW Project
Black revolutionary
Hung himself on African beads
Made in Hong Kong
Body still unidentified
His mama thought he was/something out of
                the electric circus or from
                Berstein's window
She got armed
Got ready to do some real dealin'
He so shocked woke up from the dead
Said "Mother, we can't make this a race
                issue."

Needed   Needed
                 black revolutionaries to go
                 North/South/East/West
                 "Natives" gettin' restless
Everybody caught that plane
Except four brothers—who were out fightin'
The real enemy
One doin' 2 to 15 for not allowin' himself to
Become another pig statistic
Another waitin' the chair "cause his rod jammed"
The third had noble intentions but his
Second in command was "The Man"
The last ended up mailin' revolutionary
Letters from New Orleans
I saw them all they still
Wondering why we
Won't do our thing
Brothers
Who
Will
Lead
Us?

True black leadership
Didn't need the chains
The plantations
The middle passage
The Romans
Saint Peter
Homer
Karl Marx

The Civil War
The Berlin Conference
True black leadership: was in Africa
                    died when "we"
                    accepted visitors
True black leadership is "the bloods," "the
                    uglies," "the bigga
                    boo's," "the illiterate,"
                    "the street niggers";
Didn't need
Prince Henry
The Bible
The rapers
The confession hearers
The middle class
The indoctrinated
Allah
The ghetto's
Bob Dylan (dig me "Sea Lion")
The dashiki wearers
Montgomery
The civil rights nonleaders
The integration seekers
True black leadership
Need's only you & me; me & you;

Black revolutionaries
Fightin'
The black masses
The frustrated against the hated/feared
                    weak

The educated controlled niggers
Against the black ugly masses
The power hungry against the powerless
The afro wearers against the wig bearers
The hope becoming the hopeless
Contrary to "party line"
We have more to fight for than a piece
                              of pie
Or the end of capitalism
That some jive ass tune
So often played
By the NAACP, NUL, CORE, even the W.E.B.
                    Dubois Clubs—old Dubois must
                    be "trippin' " in his grave

And now it's finally
Got all us niggers
Runnin' crazy tryin' to
Steal airplanes to Cuba, move to Suburbia
A
Whole race
Of people moved
At the expense of TWA
Will the real
Karl Marx
Show himself
And
Choose a prize
You have
Finally done what Marcus Garvey
Couldn't do

Black revolutionary
Got his pad
In Greenwich Village
Next to a white
Girl named Sue
If you want him
You gotta' go up
Sue's ass too
His face so far in shit even he can't
                              find it
Brothers
Who
Will
Lead
Us?

China gotta' new Marco Polo
He's multi-colored/has middle class status
                    but thinks he's one of the masses/
                    degree in Afro-American History
                    from Harvard
Saw him the other day in the village
Sellin' Panther Posters—to "the masses"

                    (of white liberals
                    that is)

African dressed
"Red book in pocket"
Sister on arm—who wears expensive
                    Leslie Uggam's afro wig
                    (almost looked real even
                    fooled me)

Well schooled in Marxist theories
Join the do-nothings club
& don't expect more than your
Normal supply of weed
Your picture in EBONY
A village apartment (lower eastside
                             that is)
The true black leaders
Are being captured
Sentenced
& imprisoned
Exactly
In this
Order
I will miss
The thrill
Of hearing
Them
"Rap"
Brothers
Have you
Ever
thought
About
Following
Yourselves?????

TIMOTHY L. PORTER

"Now in the black"

Now in the
black,
after birth before
death
womb
of the old man's farm,
in the deepest
star and country
open sweet smell
of an Indian summer,
all labor,
all sensation
has ceased—must be
supplanted by our song, while
our brother
leaves the farm which
once belonged
but now is left,
forgotten or
half-remembered,
lost like
dead summers,
silent in shades of
many-mooned and mirrored nights,
echoing the voice which once

announced that
here
life's harvest and grain
harbored in his silos.

The worn-out old man
has left for city lust.

Another city-dirty day
begins.
With its harlot's call to
day life, the sun,
ascending the
harbor's city,
ablaze with indignation,
making up for the negation that
night
wrought last,
excites the waters and the sky,
casts darkened remembrances of night
over ships' sides,
skips lustfully,
glitteringly, hungrily,
with pocket-book in hand and haste hip whore steps,
over the five-thirty A.M.
summer spires and scrappers,
opens the city's womb.

Summer makes the face of life so
unreserved and so
piercing,
catching the old man

moving through the dim
city street where
the mighty stench of
these and many a
thrown can half-
empty with beer blends
reeking, with whispering
silence,
to end,
to see,
to ressurrect itself
and him.

and the smell of warm
summer rain on
an old felt hat, while
the city laughs at
him again.

Old man, trying—
to hold the force which
catches sound to
breathe
the summer air,
to catch the summer wind,
to feel the lime of
half-seen people, singing
in half-heard places,
making feeble attempts
at being born, or laughing,
all in a summer's night,
or in a people-stuffy bus

with ashen axen countenance
(ex-earth, ex-hearth)
and animalated smell and
sound of
easy rasping breath.
Now he wants milk. This one,
this old one, is
drunk, and
we all pass through
the womb of america, singing
joyfully,
lustfully,
happily,
emptily,
all on the way
to Baltimore or
Pacific coast or
northernmost hem of
your pregnant lady's dress.
And all along
a big brown face sits
on an empty box and looks
from under an old felt hat
at the young man's city.
An old manned voice
from in that face
speaks, and the lady
has no pity.

Brother, a coin, a word, a smile
and your life shall be

blessed—

a pencil for a coin
a word for a word
a smile for a smile.

Or where do you bend
when once the day has
lent itself to
dark cellars?

To wither alone
without our song.

ERIC PRIESTLEY

"Poetry"

Will never sell. Get that script out of my face.
Go to hell. Go talk to your mother.
I don't like you anyway. You're a phony.
Prefabricating a bunch of noise.
Shooting the bull with the boys.
Making anything, but music.
Pretending to really be funny.
Dumb . . . Dumb on the telephone.
Scared of women.
"Sissy," "Sapsucker," "Chump," "Rumpkin."
Playing your game on the people.
You can't act. Shut up. Don' nobody want to hear that
     "shit."
"Dat's right. If you don't dig it "split."
Who let your ass in here anyway?
I know this is goin' to be a messed-up day.
You loud, unruly, and always out of hand. You can't spell.
You smell. You never bathe.
Sittin' up here stuck on yourself, and your own stupid
     words.
Don't nobody dig your plot, or the way you play.
Quit beggin'. You'll make people hate you.
Dat's alright they already do.
I'm talkin' to you. Throw him a bone.
Ain't you got no home? Him too.

Naw! We don't want you around.
"Scram" "punk." Get out of town.
Wait a minute. Hold it. Don't "split."
Let me get one of "dem" cigarettes.
So it's your last one?
Boy you sure are sad.
How many drinks you done had?
How many skotches? How much whiskey?
How much burbon? Wine? Beer?
How many pretzels you eat today "knick-knack"?
You been droppin' them pills?
You ain't funny. Where is the "weed"?
Everything you got to say is void.
You a "paranoid sucka."
Naw! Man. I don' fool with no "smack."
Nigga's like you should be dead.
When the last time you had any sleep?
Been to bed?
Got some rest?
Man you need it.
You "sho" look bad.
Go on "make it."
Shew pest.
Go sleep in the head. Go die.
Go sleep in the "head."
Stick your "kag" in Jone's *Toilet*, and cry.
And don't start "rappin" to me 'bout what's bein' said.
Man you a "wig."
Full of that pig.
Wallering 'round here like people.

"Asshole," "Flimy," "lame," you righteous insane.
Since you won't behave, go find you a cave,
Or a crack in your beat up wall.
Get in it, and remain.
That's all . . .

Recreation

(Written in a poolhall on 41st Central)

Jazz. Muffled voices pushed behind the squeaking doors of
    a place.
Costello racking balls with tales 'bout being in King Kong.
Pulsating on the pleasant sounds of Coltrane on suprano.
Yeah! A lot of noise. Niggas' droppin' pills, sticks, and
    selling wolf tickets.
Stacked back to back in a rack of billard balls in one of the
    halls of fear.
Breakin', bumpin', and bangin' their brains out. Frozen
    faces.
Lips that twitter. Murmurs of thought that turn to shouting!
Geometrically gregarious rooms. Crowded with hungry
    faces in the monkey jungle where hustlers are hunters
    who carry guns.
Watching the flashing fumble of jagged shadows and
    figures that jig and jumble, skip and bounce off the
    walls like flies on a binge between a screen and a pane.
Everyone watching. Watching and waiting. Tasting the
    stakes hidden beneath the table, or below the neon
    lights.

While two loudly dressed heroes of the con-man forest in
the asphalt jungle proceed to chisel, and cheat each
other.
Meeting like knights from King Arthur's Court, only on
the green turf of a pocket billard table.
Poking and puncturing each other with the modern jostling
poles of mediaeval magic . . . muttering, "Play you one
for a quarter."

T. L. ROBINSON

Twang

(Part I)

blues guitar-blues people
twang twang
notes floating like water mist from a distant cloud,
like spirits from heaven.

blues guitar-blues people
twang twang twang
nurtured and tapered in bitterness
alongside the path of righteousness
where death sits waiting
hoping for some lost soul to come his way.

blues guitar-blues people
twang twang
issuing sounds like that of a woman giving birth
while her man is in jail
and her children stare with wide-eyed misery
into the icy coldness of an empty icebox
(and there's nothing colder than an empty icebox).

blues guitar-blues people
twang
twang a tune for a lost soul,
twang a tune for me.
for it is I who stand teetering at the rim of insanity

burdened down with white emptiness
and hopes, and twang
and twang,
and dreams that evaporated into thin air
along with yesterday morning's dew..........

blues guitar-blues people
twang
spread your love all over me,
cover my soul with unspeakable joy,
let me hear your groans,
let me feel your pain,
let me laugh your laughter,
let me enter your sacred wound
and bathe in the black blood
of kings that never knew no throne
and never wore no crown.

blues guitar-blues people
twang twang twang
notes floating like water mist from a distant cloud,
like spirits from heaven.
you are my sin.
you are my salvation.
you twang the story of my life.

(Part II)

blues guitar-blues people
twang twang
the silence of a man
hung down near a wall,
with moments of time

running in black streaks
staring from the shadowy depths
of a hole in the wall.

blues guitar-blues people
twang twang twang
twanging from the soul
of a now awakened ghost
sitting on a crate
justa sippin' that wine,
with the aftermath of tomorrow
staring him in the face
from a hole in the wall.

blues guitar-blues people
twang
twang a tune for a silent man,
twang a tune for me,
for it is I who stare
from the whole in the wall
seeking to cut somebody's throat,
and destroy, and twang
and twang,
and create new notes
for the constant revitalization
of the blues guitar,
and new notes
for the emergence
of the forgotten blues people.

CAROLYN M. RODGERS

Newark, For Now (68)

second-hand sights, like crumpled
mud-smudged postcards
buildings leaning on-towards each
and other, weight of sweat/rocked
bodies, pressing on/out/down
chips of red, blue, black & chalky
rubble that decorate the streets and
nourish hunger-dumb blacklings.

streets. splinters of pavements
lining puddles of dirt. pot-bellied
tubs like giant naked beer cans, frothy with
maggots, packed with rats dining on
last month's french fries.

Newark. 68. and a camel walking breeze
bumps the air with summer perfumes of
piss & hot dogs & eye-talian sausages. But somewhere,

from the lips of the night Sam Cooke's
sweet aria flows, "i know, I know i
know a chaaaaaaanj gonna shur-lee
cooooooom . . ."

A Non Poem about Vietnam

or (Try Black)

1.

I have been asked to write a poem about
Vietnam. I have been asked to label my-
self, (as if I am a brandless jar), as "pro"
or "con," on the War.

2.

I have been coaxed to deliver an opinion
About our black boys who, though still so
young they forget to wipe the milk from
their mouths, are being flown in
silver super jets to hot dark swamps, to
fight spiked booby traps and other brown-skinned
powerless people.

3.

Someone has even asked me to elaborate on the
idea of a Black boy/man fighting for a red/
white & blue democracy. It is difficult to
separate the answers from my feelings and tears,
and record on paper anything that is waterless
or sane.
But I have been told to "deal with the question
sensibly."

4.

Therefore, I have summed up my sane/opinion/
comment/statement/using 50 words, or less—

It is this:

> "no black man (or negro) should fight the
> hunkie's war, cause everytime we kill a
> Vietnamese, we are widening the crack in
> our own asses for the hunkie to shove his
> foot into."

I hope that this opinion/comment/statement
makes
my label clear.

Eulogy

my mother and
     sisters
are mourning
     the passing of a
white-haired lady, a
property-fertilized
     flower
my aunt, who has been
wilting on porches and
rocking chairs, for
twenty years (at least)
     while
piecing quilts and
humming hymns. me
and my sisters
never even smelled her,

she never blossomed in our lives but the
    talk
of her could have descented a
skunk-filled swamp; shewasrich (!) i
    knew
of her.

                    i wonder if
my mother and
    sisters
will weep
    for the
city rockers, the
poverty-pollinated weeds who burst into
    affirming flames in Detroit
who in five days
passed (i mean died), lite (i mean burned),
white minds (i mean lies)
i mean (how)
    do you mourn
for
    people
you never begged or bragged with
    except that
maybe you could if a
    hammer
had ever chiseled you out a
    black
    soul. brothers.
my mother and
    sisters

are mourning.
　　　　how shall we
burn their tears?

U Name This One

let uh revolution come. uh
state of peace is not known to me
anyway
since i grew uhround in chi town
where
howlin wolf howled in the tavern on 47th st.
and muddy waters made u cry the salty nigger blues,
　　　where pee wee cut lonnel fuh fuckin wid
　　　his sistuh and blood baptized the street
　　　at least twice ev'ry week and judy got
　　　kicked outa grammar school fuh bein pregnant
　　　and died tryin to ungrow the seed
　　　　　we was all up in there and
　　　　　just livin was guerilla warfare, yeah.

let uh revolution come.
couldn't be no action like what
i dun already seen.

Jesus Was Crucified or:
It Must Be Deep

(an epic pome)

i was sick
and my motha called me
tonight yeah, she did she
sd she was sorri
i was sick, but what
  she wanted tuh tell
me was that i shud pray or
have her (hunky) preacher
pray fuh me, she sd. i
had too much hate in me
she sd u know the way yuh think is
got a lots to do
wid the way u feel, and i
agreed, told her i WAS angry a lot THESE days
and maybe my insides was too and she sd
        why it's somethin wrong wid yo mind girl
that's what it is
                and i sd yes, i was aware a lot
lately and she sd if she had evah known educashun
woulda mad me crazi, she woulda neva sent me to
school (college that is)
she sd the way i worked my fingers to the bone in
this white mans factori to make u a de-cent some-
bodi and here u are actin not like decent folks
        talkin bout hatin white folks & revolution
& such and runnin round wid Negroes
        WHO CURSE IN PUBLIC!!! (she sd)
THEY COMMUNIST GIRL!!! DON'T YUH KNOW

THAT???
   DON'T YUH READ*THE NEWSPAPERS??????
                                   (and i sd)
i don't believe—(and she sd) U DON'T BELIEVE IN
                          GOD NO MO DO U?????
u wudn't raised that way! U gon die and go tuh HELL
and i sd i hoped it wudn't be NO HUNKIES there
and she sd
what do u mean, there is some good white people and
some bad ones, just like there is negroes
and i says i had neva seen ONE (wite good that is) but
she sd negroes ain't redi, i knows this and
deep in yo heart you do too and i sd yes u right
negroes ain't readi and she sd
why just the utha day i was in the store and there was
uh negro packin clerk put uh colored woman's ice cream
in her grocery bag widout wun of them "don't melt" bags
    and the colored ladi sd to the colored clerk
"how do u know mah ice cream ain't gon tuh melt befo I
git home."
                  clerk sd. "i don't" and took the ice cream
                  back out and put it in wun of them "stay hard"
                  bags
and me and that ladi sd see, ne-groes don't treat
nobody right why that clerk packin groceries was un
grown main, acted mad. white folks wudn't treat yuh that
way. why when i went tuh the BANK the otha day to de-
posit some MONEY
this white man helped me fast and nice. u gon die girl
and go tuh hell if yuh hate white folks. i sd, me and
my friends could dig it . . . hell, that is

she sd du u pray? i sd sorta when i hear Coltrane and
she sd if yuh read yuh bible it'll show u read genesis
revelation and she couldn't remember the otha chapter
i should read but she sd what was in the Bible was
happnin now, fire & all and she sd just cause i didn't
 believe the bible don't make it not true
      (and i sd)
 just cause she believed the bible didn't make it true
and she sd it is it is and deep deep down
in yo heart u know it's true
      (and i sd)

  it must be deeep
she sd i gon pray fuh u tuh be saved. i sd thank yuh
  but befo she hung up my motha sd
  well girl, if yuh need me call me
i hope we don't have to straighten the truth out no mo.
i sd i hoped we didn't too
    (it was 10 P.M. when she called)
she sd, i got tuh go so i can git up early tomorrow
and go tuh the social security board to clarify my
record cause i need my money.
work hard for 30 yrs. and they don't want tuh give me
$28.00 once every two weeks.
   i sd yeah . . .
don't let em nail u wid no technicalities
  git yo checks . . . (then i sd)

  catch yuh later on Jesus, i mean motha!
   it must be
     deeeeep. . . .

SONIA SANCHEZ

right on: white america

this country might have
been a pio
                neer land
once.
but.   there ain't
no mo
      indians   blowing
custer's mind
            with a different
image of america.
                        this country
might have
            needed shoot/
outs/daily/
      once.
            but. there ain't
no mo real/white/   allamerican
                        bad/guys.
just.
      u & me.
            blk/and un/armed.
this country might have
been a pion
            eer land.   once.
                        and it still is.

check out
          the fallling
gun/shells   on our blk/tomorrows.

RUBY C. SAUNDERS

Lawd, Dese Colored Chillum

I get my degree
The Spring of '52
Walked all over this town.

Got a Brooks Brothers' suit
Shoes brand new
I was gonna knock the Whiteman down.

I had learned me some languages too
French I.
And French II.
Got a *bad* hat or two.

Finally got a job The Winter of '52

I practiced in the mirror
Knew just what to do
How to act like Charley
And speak like him too.

I left home early
In the morningtime
Proud as I could be
Whitewashed
Grinning
9-to-5
Bluecollar
Job
Me.

A nappy-headed boy
Some son of a mother . . .
Said
        "HEY, BROTHER!"
Lawd, dese Colored chillum won't let you be
White for nothing.

Don't Pay

I went to the place
They had marked on my card.
I said
My name is
My numbers are
I want to draw my unemployment insurance.

The lady said
Wait! have a seat over there
We have to call your job
Fill out the form ignore race
Some people act like they own the place.

I waited long . . .
You come in every Thursday . . . she said.
Same old game going on and on.

I went back Thursday before five.
My job had said . . . I quit . . . they don't know why.
I told that agent that's a lie.
I wore my hair in an African-do

My boss said
Straighten it or you're through.

I said "fuck you"

Them white girls come in here
Looking like Sampson. Hair hanging straight covering
Their faces.
But when I'm natural . . . I'm wrong!
Well . . . fuck you, Johnny, all night long!

That's how come I ain't got no job.
My name is
My numbers are
I want to draw my unemployment insurance.

Be Natural, Baby

My process had regressed, in the last couple of
Weeks. My conk had seen it's day. My boys were
All over my ass. Be natural, baby, they would say.

Cut me an Afro the other day. Man, that was a sight.
Hair going every which a way. Nothing came out right.
I went to work, Monday, trying to be cool, knowing
I had to fight those crackers like a fool.
Well, the crackers were peeking . . . and the Toms
Didn't know what to say. I kept real busy and
Got through the day.

I got my thing together. Carried Kenyetta on the train.
I read a little Stokely too! You should have seen me
Running my game! I moved into the city. Brought me some
Pot and stuff. I smoked with the good guys. I knew I was
Tough! . . . Knew I was tough! I would run down the game
On the black revolution . . . I ran down the story on
The ultimate solution! . . . I got high . . . I got high, baby!
And settled back! Pulled out my metaphysical meditations
And started working that white monkey off my back.
"Ran my fingers through Miss Ann's hair. Eased my hand
Up her thigh!"
I'm black and beautiful!
Got me a dashiki and shit!
My 'fro' is together! . . . I'm clean. Can you dig it!

The Generation Gap

I takes up for my colored men
Let me tell you, chile
I takes up for me colored men
Been doing it for quite a while.

I don't let these whitefolks tell me
Nothing!
Jesus Christ above
Anything that Rap Brown does
He's doing it out of love.

I turns on my TV set
Cause my FM needs some fixing

I hears the news everyday
Just to see what Charley be thinking.

Don't you show no disrespect
Standing in my face.
Jesus Christ lawd's my saviour
Colored men got lots to take.
And they takes it too
I tell you
They takes it too
I say
Sing their praises bless the lawd
Makes me want to shout!

I don't wear my hair all nappy
Don't throw my fists up in the air
I can't wear them African garments
On my subway job, no how.
But I knows that
You's in colleges and schools
All over this land
Got good job and houses, senators,
Congressmen, the vote . . . plans!
Now just because this is so
And the white folks calls you news
Remember . . . Tom . . . and . . . Aunt Jemima
Bent low to pay your dues.

My Man Was Here Today

I meant to scrub my floors . . .
Wash my hair . . . do my nails.
Soak in some "desert flower" . . .
But he called . . .
Sweet talkin' and jivin' about coming over!
I took a shower.

Auditions

How many niggers did you say were out there?
Four.
Give classic ballet as a starter . . .
If they can do that
Make 'em walk on water!

JOHNIE SCOTT

A Short Poem for Frustrated Poets
(*kudos for the men who made it thru*)

ain't too much happening around town anymore
    now that most of the fellas done finished what they
        started out
and seen that it wasn't no more they could do
    so they packed bags, suitcases and boxes
loaded up on plenty of the best hashish available
    and then split seeking to find new Meccas of revolution.

discontent was a perishable commodity around these parts.
    once the fellas had gone off as deeply into it as they
        could
they found this out and rather than take time to wonder
        why
    (we all knew the answers, believe me, we all knew)
everybody got hat, coattails flapping in the wind,
    and now it looks like it's just me and a few others left
        around here.

after a while it becomes a drag changing records,
    or even going out to buy new records to put on the
        turntable.
don't care if it's jazz you're talking about or thinking of,
    don't care if it's Miles, Monk, Coltrane, Eric Dolphy,
        or John Handy.

don't care if it's blues that's on the box,
　　cause listening to the blues can be depressing too.

born under a bad sign
　　who's making love to your old lady while you are out
　　　　making love
you're all I need
　　the tracks of my tears, oh, I wish it would rain,
sometimes I feel like a motherless child,
　　they call it stormy monday but tuesday's just as bad.

get to the point where you're tired of knowing every line
　　to every blues
　　that was ever recorded anywhere in this country by
　　Black people.
get to the point where you get tired of reading all the
　　BLACK BOOKS, yes,
　　tired of knowing how well BLACK PEOPLE have
　　been fucked around, yes
tired of knowing better than the teacher knows the story
　　and how it goes,
　　tired of sounding original about hard shit that hap-
　　pened long ago.

it comes, this feeling, and now that it is here I might as
　　well confess:
　　confess to the sin of trying myself to be blacker than
　　black
confess to the sin of trying myself to be poorer than poor
　　confess to the sin of trying myself to be more righteous
　　than right
confess to the sin myself of trying to be cooler than cool

confess, confess, confess, time and time and time
   again.
and why? Because it is true.
   everything, all of this is true.
and being alone, why I ain't no more alone than the next
      man.
   maybe just as alone, but then that's my frustration
      showing
the fact that I dwell on the topic of loneliness. why is it
      that so many
   black poets are hung-up on just being super-duper hip
      shit and
all the jive vernacular that goes along with it?

why? I want to know cause right now in my life I got's to
      face facts
   like the meaning of my woman in my life, the meaning
      of being a father.
the meaning of being a provider, cause none of it is
      abstract bullshit
   no more that I can put off on pages and hope,
      seriously, that
it dies there. more than that, that it dies without being
      seen by you.

What Poetry is for Me

A few short words on the subject. Poetry is Charlie Mingus on the sides that never caught the public's attention. And it was not groovy (not even now) to say so. Poetry is John Coltrane forever sounding good (with jams like OM, COSMIC TRANE, OLE, MATING CALL, ASCENSION, MY FAVORITE THINGS, all of these still sounding good). Poetry is being able to give Smokey Robinson his full due as a poet. To recognize in "The Tracks of Mye Tears," "Beauty's Only Skin Deep," and "My Girl Has Gone" poetical genius. And being able to stand by what I have just said. The courage. You understand, the courage which goes with standing by those young black brothers on the street corners and in the pool halls all across the country, who will say that they knew this all the time. Which makes what I say very unoriginal but nevertheless something I believe in and so hold to as the truth. Poetry is all the rest—you know, the old-timers reminiscing about Billie Holiday and Bessie Smith and Florence West, the "Lil' Nightingale." The strength these women gave to Black Men with no other way to go but down. Poetry is a man writing just to be writing and not for the times, or for everlasting glory or fame, which, after all is said and done, even my pitifully vain ego has to admit is only temporary. Poetry is not words, or sentences well constructed. It is not finishing college Phi Beta Kappa and Magna Cum Laude. It is not being bourgeoise or wealthy or poor. It is more than these, Things. Poetry is, Spirit. Not just something, the ah-ha you say when searching for a way out of the darkness. Poetry is knowing that the magic lantern is just one more way of saying that hope moves on and on. Poetry is, it belongs to people. Yes. And the Indians, the Kahlil Gibrans and Tagores and all the rest had their fingers on it long before the Western world ever got their bloodied hands on it. Poetry is what black kids raise their eyes to once they close the book handed them in public schools and start thinking for themselves. Poetry is all of this, and it is so much more. But it is, above all, Force. And, check this—*Poetry cannot be fucked with.* Those who don't know will soon find this out. Poetry is the People, the way we want to be.

Poem for Joyce

my words are sad notes best tossed aside
    against the day when the Trashman comes to pick up
    trash.
remember me for my words for they are all I have
    in this world of ours, this land of plenty where the
government can dump millions of dollars of wheat
    into the sea.

remember me for my words, Joyce,
    for they are all that I can give you.
I don't have to tell you that I'm poor.
    we both know that, and more, as quiet as it's kept.

I'm poor, yes, and I'm black, yes, and I live in the ghetto,
    yes, but that don't, no, it don't give me no complex.

you see, Joyce,
    if I wanted to, I could be pretty and fancy and all that.
I could sit back in a chair for hours
    and talk to you, if nothing else, then just about
what it really means to have someone like you
    sticking here in my corner knowing that I'm down and
        out.

don't really care to cop a poor mouth,
    cause that really ain't where I'm coming from.
don't care actually to keep fronting
    like I got something and I ain't got shit worth count-
        ing.
Joyce, I ain't got nothing, Baby,
    I ain't got nothing to offer you but me.
I love you, Joyce,
    I love you so much until sometimes it scares me.
I sit and I think and I stare at you
    and when I think that you might be staring at me
why, I get shamed and start blushing and going through
        changes
    no other girl under the sun done ever put me thru.

I mean,
    like I don't go out of my way looking for trips to go on.
cause the world has got enough of those to go around.

you know what?
    it comes to this:
me, by myself now,

      and it ain't nobody looking over my shoulder making
      me

write this poem to you.

it ain't nobody that done asked me if I ever wrote any love poems. no. it ain't none of that kinda funny-style shit.

this is me.

nothing, if you want to see me that way.

but this is me.

and I see now that I'll never love another.

let me be sweet to you.

let me be good to you.

let me hold you, yes!

let me hold you and squeeze you,

or maybe even just touch you,

but just let me do that

and I'll be just fine.

know what, Joyce?

know what I saw yesterday

while I was out in those streets

begging pennies from lint-lined pockets

playing the role of the puppet-sized gourmet

at a wine-stained oaken table and generally

just tripping out very heavy

had you on my mind alla da time.
thinking bout you, bout how nice
it would be to come home to you,
to come to your loving arms and
go to sleep happy cause if I ain't
got nothing else at least I got
my woman.

thass why I'm writing you this poem, Joyce.
    because there's a lotta times when I get hung-up,
yes, get hung-up in a whole lotta bullshit
        that don't no kinda way make no sense and you and I
          both
know it,
               (but you let me slide,
                 let me ease on off for the next day)
listening to my footsteps hollowly echoing
    dark the alleyway down the alleyway there I go
not quite being able to see what's right in front of me
    but moving on ahead anyway cause thass the bizness
a man's gotta involve hisself inta nowadays otherways,
                              Missy,
it ain't too much that really means anything.

not people.
not money.
not fine homes or long cars or who got the most bombs.
not none of that shit.
not you.
not me.
not nothing, Baby, but what we got going for ourselves.

I want more than just the Blues, Joyce.
I want my Baby. I want Her Love, Her Tears, Her Happi-
    ness.
I want to make my Baby happy. I want to make you
    happy.
Will you make me Happy, too?

SAUNDRA SHARP

Reaching Back

I keep reaching back for the magic of those first few days
    when we found each other.
When we discovered that we both liked mayonnaise on
    hamburgers medium well done,
And neither had ever read *Wuthering Heights*.
When we concurred on the agonies of war and disagreed
    about the importance of being earnest.

When your touch was gentle, and your eyes bright
As you told me about taking over new york city before it
    overtook you.
When you ran your fingers softly through my hair,
Asking if it was all right to mess it up
And needing no answer.
When I made you laugh,
And your laughing made me feel good.

I keep reaching back for that exact moment when you
    reached for me
And I came into your arms for our first kiss—
Hesitant, unsure, afraid to be too eager,
Very happy to be there.

This fairy tale gone bad,
This sweep spring fruit withered before ripening—

Is it that the flower blossoms too quickly, and therefore
    closes too soon?

Or are we too strongly molded in our separate worlds?

I keep reaching back, reaching back for the magic of those
    first days when we found each other.

I keep reaching back,
               and grasping—
                          nothing.

A Seeing Eye-Dog

There is no need to flirt with him today.
I'm barefoot,
And my blue jeans are comfortable
And my long red cape is a groove.
My hair is together,
And my face is clean.
I'm sitting on a rock by the water
Feeding swans,
Letting the sun glow warmly on my brown skin.
And I'm singing inside—
He would not notice.

On any given tomorrow I could walk into his office:
High hems and heels,
Hips and red lips,
Hair in Henri of Paris curls,
Fluorescent lights glowing on my
Air-conditioned, twice powdered skin.
There would be no need to flirt with him that day—

For he would come, lap-dog style,
A bright-eyed, bushy-tailed,
Panting Mr. Cool,
and "When can we have dinner together?"

He tells all the fellows he's an
Expert on female beauty.

DAN SIMMONS

Nationalism

I never knew Jews could show such
chauvinism or relish bloodletting until
Israel lived.

Such devotion keeps me awake and
bids me dream:

Where is that stretch of land, rock
and hill or dune of sand
Where Afro-Americans can purpose
gain
And strike a blow for freedom that
will not be lost to muffled concepts,
gradualism, poverty programs, Western
democracy and Jesus Christ?

SHIRLEY STAPLES

"Getting It Together"

i have awakened
from my dream world
of reactionary flowers
and have clothed
myself in fibres of liberation
upon my head
I have placed
the garland of revolution
    Poets spoke
    of wars
    and brothers
    rapped
    away the time
    and all i could do
    was speak of
    white roses
    and daisies
    crosses were being burned—
    justice was being denied
    bullets were stilling lives
    and yet i marvelled at
    unrealistic
    flower gardens
    until
        WEEDS

of Don Lee, Ameer Baraka, Giovanni, Pfister
    and others made
    my rose petals wither
    and the thorns
    of the rose
    pricked
    my finger
    and i saw real blood
i speak no more of white lilies
and the magnolias no longer smell sweet
my reactionary flower world
    is non-existant
    and i listen
    as the revolutionary
    Weeds of Reality
rap to me
and as the
last wilted flower
dries up in
the sands of changing times
i get my thing Together.

A Sister Speaks of Rapping

    When
      I
    Rap...
      I do

it so
discreetly
And it
comes
out so
sweetly
Like
Black
Honey/Gold
It
Affects
you
When it is
least
Expected to
I am
told
But
don't
ever
take
my
Rap
Just
for
a
Rap
Because
It's
Coming

Straight
From
My
Heart
The
Message
Is
Like
Fine
And it
Burns.
Listen
Closely
Hear the
Silky-Smooth
Drawl?
It will
quietly
but
eventually
blow
your
Mind . . .

GLENN STOKES

Blue Texarkana

the whaling backdoor of Texarkana
    back there in the old
cottonfields back home
    back in the garden
of the gruesome descent
   to the hay shed and potato
peels the invisible highway
      and fall
  of the high gods
             from Jackson to Selma
to wine bottles on a back
    wooden porch and moonshine
crystallizing on dust on mantel
pictures of old dad and poor momma

who flipped out popping
questions into my discriminating head
    because the clay was too Red
    in Columbus that spring so
Injuns rose from the gullies
and slipped knives between my
    aching shoulder blades
    making love mercy black-eyed pudding
steeple-chased milk and contraceptives
to curve overproductive minds

and turn black molasses to weak wine
        potato wine on my uncle's back porch
his fish bubbling at the mouth
in their pond which reflects everything
        hidden and usually obscured
        never seeing dusty Texarkana and
        fudge-faced pie with death
on their hands
it was Texarkana hell
and southern belles ringing in my
        ear drums I hated
        could not stand found my love
        thrusted down
        down down
my gasping throat

to think to know to guess
that home they died a
thousand whaling times on trees
        tombstones broken chimneys of grass
        brick and dust porch tracts
        mosquito heaps their carcasses
laughing not being "human"
they died we forgot but
cannot filter from our bloods
        the trueness the arrowness
        lying in this closet-shaped town
        we cannot remove the stink

ROBERT L. TERRELL

For Frantz Fanon

I
have heard the Word
BROTHER
And:
have begun to stoke the smoldering kilns
to stealthily stow the glistening
SILVER SPEARS
My mask scarce hides my
PUTRID CANCEROUS RAGE
Yet:
My sights remain clear!
even as I stir these
PUNGENT COCKTAILS
Yes:
I now understand
the prophetic White Hot Sun
which at the coming of Night
turns BLOOD RED
and flows from the bleeding sky
Sinking into
BLACKNESS BEAUTIFUL

CHARLES THOMAS

In Search of a God

They require of us a song,
But where are our Gods?
Did we leave them on the shores
   of Africa?

Could the name of Olorun,
   the highest God,
be shouted across icy waters,
His omnipresence felt
as one gazed from the auction block
into the brutal masks of alien faces?

Did one dare evoke Shango
to rain down his fiery wrath
on the tormentors of blackness,
reveling in their repulsive wrath
grown ripe and ready to be loosed
on a magnificent race of men

   who
made stride across the continent of Africa
keeping steady gait thru the tangled jungles
   who
with sanded eyes
treaded the vast Sahara and roamed the Kalahari
   who
climbed Mt. Cameroon and Kilimanjaro

encircled by ancestral dieties
            who
rowed with muscular rhythm
along the Zambezi and the Nile?

Would Ogun, God of Iron,
            descend from heaven
            on a spider's web
            and with his axe of iron
            cut the tyrants loose
            from his suffering people?

And Okun, with coral dress
            and mudfish legs,
Would he disturb the sea
and receive his lost leaping children
from the wretched vessels that brought them to Hell
            from a land of the free?

            Still lost
        in an alien world
    we raise our black voices
    across the bloody sea,
Spirits! Gods! or whatever
            You be!

Aiwel,
        Ala,
            Amma,
                Gu!

Kibuka,
        Ngewo,

Nyame,
Mawu!

Musa,
Zin,
Mulungu,
Chuckwu!

Cover Us . . . . . !
Deliver Us . . . !

UHURU!

Ode to the Smiths:
Bessie, Mamie, Laura, Clara and Trixie
(The Original Sisters of Soul)

Oh joyous cantor!
(not of the synagogue)
Oh sweet Blackbird of song!
Where did you get your style?

In
the converted basement
of Ebenezar Baptist Church . . .
Or in the lofty choir stands of
Mt. Zion?

Did Miss Prudence Purselips
pound out your key
on
a 19th century console? . .

Or
did the Rev. T. D. Jackson
inspire you
to raise a Sunday Morning song?

Was it the hyperrhythms
of high-heeled shoes
being stamped on the floor
by
Sister Hawkins?
Or
the bucolic bass of Brother Simmons
moaning
a deep Amen. . . ?

Whatever it was,
it sure struck your soul!

So sing on sweet sister,
SWING!
Yours is an authentic style
equalling the acrobats of a coot,
swimming and diving and floating
on quarter tones
of a blues salute.

Flat that seventh!
Ripple down to the third . . .
Let us hear a boss "blue" note!
Spread your charm in AAB form
From some lonesome lines of verse.

Man done gone—Got nowhere to go,
Man done gone—Got nowhere to go,

He left me standin', on the cold, cold, flo

Oh, it takes me back
to
Congo Square!
Where they say it all began.
When Black Blues Queens
reigned supreme . . .
Deep in the heart
of
New Orleans.

JAMES W. THOMPSON

Arms & Exit

We were taken
by armed force
(5 plain/6 uniformed
        and several cars/
        marked & plain)
from Max's K.C.—
        17th & Park Avenue
South, of course—
our diamond thoughts
        frosting in interrogations.

I thought we'd broken
        some sound barrier,
        (our language leapt
colliding with the throng
of tongues exploding
        in the room);
It was the other:
        we were varied
        much too bright
still during the hush
        I heard James Brown
("Caint stand it . . .")
the cops were taking us on.

A waiter had
        warned us

with a note:
    "Silent Week
    Holy WeeK"
King was dead!
    Slaughtered.
How could our chorus
    frighten—our language
        leapt!
Bergman had battered us.
    His Wolfe: the Freudian
flagellants sachel of superficial sins;
a small sickness seeking justification
as the innocence of ignorance,
        a genteel death.
          (Caint stand it . . .)
But innocence comes
when wisdom has won
the living/who never
    assume a willing zombie
        for social success.
        (Caint stand it . . .)
Time hadn't taken us out
the cops were taking us on.

Detective Matera
    gray haired & bold,
        as all cops are,
kept his hand upon his gun.
    Cosmos crescendoed
    "It's not my car . . .
        so what."

"Let's step outside."
"We'll all go together,"
        I'd flourished,
arranging my mind
to acceptances/
        dinner & drink
        interrupted
the car we came in
        accused of being used
in the shooting of a cop.
        (Caint stand it ...)
The cops were taking us on.

Passed diners in costumes
        faces gussied up
        in macabre projections
                as they gaped—
our procession triumphal.
Jeanne, Cecil, Cosmos, Laureta
and I—all splendiforous
        between Bulls in blue.
                The brass of buttons,
                        a complement
to my ensemble—
        Beige & Gold
against my lovely brown,
the scene was bringing
                me down;
but the cops
        were taking us on.

Tall Paul,
(insanity
    winking in his eyes
        had kissed my hand,
           teethed upon my arm,
    held tightly in
        his husky palm)
    showed joy
at our alarm:
trailed the triumphal march
    was not allowed
        to join us
    in a squad car.
    (Caint stand it ...)
And none of us looking victims
    being victimized
by bold Bulls in blue
        moving us on.

My jewelled box
    crammed with *smoke*,
        my head turned,
a *Watts* of articulated sounds:
(sirens, screams, swift shadowy shapes
    & sheaths of flame,
        a hose's hissing stream)
        sensed *their* number,
        danger, suddenly,
when Jeanne, clasping her head
    bending, screamed, "James ...

I don't want to get in that car . . .
   with HIM!"—meaning the thug
masquerading in plainclothes
   w/pock-marked face &
       bleary eyes, struggling
          from sleep to shift
             on the back seat.
We were given to uniformed men
   and rode in a regular
       marked car w/irregular
          Bulls in blue,
             who were polite—
                for once!
          (It's the REPORT.)
They took us on;
   told Paul to walk
       and delivered directions;
my mind made a minute
          vivisection of the scene.
Color of eyes/or color of hair
   what was it that kept him
       from being where
          we were, and why/when joy
had brought him to the gate
          did they shut it—
             make him wait & walk—
                he was too eager
                   to be "in!"
Life's a clutter of cool men,
       frozen out
          but eager to be "in!"

The cops had taken us on.

21st Precinct—
      one flight up
        we came to rest,
flowering in florescent light;
our plumage definitely out of place
      in the sterile shine
        of the L-shaped polished room,
more a corridor of things: desks, typewriters,
chairs, cabinets, a cell—
          all color co-ordinated to create
            cold despair,
a weakening of one's will—
        our language leapt!
      We bloomed.
The cops were doomed
      to respond. Their frosted
pleasantness was a discipline
      for them.
Having taken us out—
      they were forced to take us on.

We waited turns
      to give our names
        & numbers
but not our occupations—
Detective Matera & the clean-cut
      Goldwater Negro, overacting
        in his scene,
did the questioning. Cosmos, gleamed

w/anger—a mantling of fear.
      Paul bounded, smiling, up the stairs
        to rest at my side.
I was enthroned upon the
      samsonite surface of a
          gray metal desk,
lifted, legs crossed, in a pure prospective
        of the scene, my jeweled box
            crammed w/*smoke* was fire
              in my fist—
"Can I Get a Witness," the melody
        mounting in my mind;
And the buff cell whose sign
        ordered:
              NO SMOKING
              TALKING
              DRINKING
                FOOD NOT ALLOWED
        nothing there to sit on
        but the polished floor
(prisoners are supposed to stand.)
              NO HANGING ON THE BARS
              ALLOWED
            nothing given.
After an informal
      line-up in a room
        w/a view
        for the witnesses,
we were released—
        w/nothing given—
        no apologies,

definitely, NO APOLOGIES;
Time hadn't taken us out,
          the cops had taken us on.

Beauty Then Is Being

Saturday afternoon and sun—sifting,
filtered through gems of latticed dust
veiling the panes of my apt.'s eyes, listing
First Avenue. And sounds of Cecil just
awakening beneath the eaves (having placed
my speakers but a foot's imagined thrust
from the ceiling on an oaken shelf, faced
with art objects—in tribute to the sounds
that their volumed voices sing, spaced
as they are according to the rule), lifting
the Saturday in a sun-sound for the jewel rising
in me. Love is then fluidity fused in rust.
It is the vital in man attuned, in which trust
turns to solve the mystery of growth—not traced
—but actual in the now of being;
that, then, is the body and the mind, seeing
where it's at today. Saturday afternoon
and sun, and somewhere a body bites another tune
in Viet Nam where they tell me integration soon
is at its best, and blacks are being understood.

Mock Pop Forsooth: a tale of life and death

And saxaphones were oboes become bassoon,
fingered strings the ravished tension of the time
winged into feeling born of the song—impulsed
in a tension for the time. And the time is now
spoke the mallet, on the tight white carcass
of the drum, and the time is now, said the saxaphone
in a soprano hosanna to the bass, and the time is now
screamed the bass climbing to contralto key;
Ah, the time, was the digital pianissimo
in a fusion floating free.

Weeks later, the woman Martha
said to me, "Have you noticed
how everything foams? Detergents foam,
soap foams, lotions, hair sprays, and ammonia
foam. Posner's creamed reverse permanent
foams; everything that's instant foams:
coffee, tea, milk, even mashed potatoes,
juices, soups, frozen creamed tomatoes.
And the water foams. Fuel forcing rockets
into orbit foams. Have you seen the sea
on T.V. in those Pepsi ads? Even people foam."
But she didn't say, people not of the present foam,
or that LSD is a foamy film trip for freaks
searching for a time to be in. I am of the
present—I ferment but I do not foam.

The piano in motive solo
led saxes to become, all horn,
muscular and dark of body
carried on the muted rhythm
of the drum, fanned by the basses

climbing contralto voice. "This
is the music of the future," announced
the moderator in the present tense.
And the sound, flooding, sent his fiction
scurrying from cellar to the street.
there it hopped into the garbage of the past—
it remains, nibbling at yesterday—for the present.
"Really," she repeated. "Haven't you noticed
how everything foams?" I laughed in a high
staccato key; "Inks in presses printing the
literature foams, even epileptic historians
foam. Hoosier homosexuals foam, inadequate
heterosexuals foam. Lady Clairol foams,
shampoo, seltzer, miracle whipped margarine
foams. My dear, whatever fogs is foam.
I live to see, so I'm going home.
Madame, I am of the present—
I ferment but I do not foam."

QUINCY TROUPE

A Splib Odyssey

From the basement of an opportunist's slave ship. A studio apartment 3 feet high by 4 feet wide by 6 feet long. Nigger inside, pitchin an rollin in his own shit and vomit—coming to a new land, a new rhythm . . . Strong, docile, dumb, unwashed, Black Angus Cattle Chattel, fallen early in the hands of Seekers, Grabbers and Carp-faced Speculators.

"The market will bear five dollars a pound for strong bucks with good teeth, three-fifty a pound for fertile females."

Thus the prophecy of bondage began . . .

Quickly, enterprising entrepreners, hip on Nigger Husbandry and slash-whip-cracking, created a sound economy based upon new principles of cotton pickin. Nat Turner staged a light-weight coup got busted and hanged—A precedent, a portent . . .

Introduction of the Cat O Nine in the pickin and plantin industry improved the learning curve 25%, and night chains in the chatterly reduced the dropout rate 37%, yielding sufficient bales of fluffy white irony to cure the unemployment problem in the North, and finance the first holy war.

The war of independence—yeah . . .

The Blackfolks toiled
Derry Derry Down

The White folks got spoiled
Derry Down Down

A few Niggers ran away
Derry Derry Down
Most had to stay
Derry Down Down

It went that way:
Down, Down, Down

TILL:

ABRAHAM JESUS LINCOLN, The Great EQUIVO-
CATOR, needing a front to start a New shoot up, Natural-
ized Nigger and set him free.

Or so they say—Uh Huh

It took twenty years for the first gig to break—that's where
Sapphire came in—strong, proud, black, burning in kitchens
on the other side of the track—selling her milk and bustin
suds—While Coons on corners played cards, and danced
to razors. Early blues . . .

Sapphire grew consistently heavier, harder—less apt to put
up with the bull shit Willy, unemployed and shuffling,
would be dealin (quiet as its kept, from the bottom of the
deck)

Thus—in time . . . a Functional Matriarchy. Sapphire was
working—you dig. Streets, yea. Unsubtle, hard black top
streets, Uh Huh, St. Lou, Chicago, New Orleans, Philly,

New York—these towns *invented* the street the Nigger's home—Tobacco Road, Catfish Row, Coon Hollow—Abrasive surfaces taking black skin, breaking black bones—a new black Gestalt . . .

Like back in the twenties when times was so hard rats was eating onions and crying cause they couldn't find cheese.

Was at this time that a new bag began—Black Genocide . . .

Unable to get into such Labor Unions as—the Mailman's, Fireman's, Policeman's, Fisherman's, Garbageman's, Trashman's, etc.—Brother ended up with a lot of time on his hands.

So he sat alot, sang alot, played alot, drank alot, smoked alot, fucked alot, gambled alot, lost Sapphire's money alot and got angry alot—you dig . . .

Like anyone would.

But the man had a plan . . .

The scam was: by systematically *reducing* the penalties provided for murders perpetrated upon the person of Nigger X by Nigger Y, the man made it attractive for coons to blow each other away.

And they did.

But it didn't matter . . .

Cause it was getting crowded on Tobacco Road and Brother didn't know who his brothers were—illegitimacy, you dig. And the shit grew Bluer and Bluer and Bluer.

Till Lady Day blew it—and Time Stood Still

And Catfish Row is called Ghetto—Uh Huh.

A hundred blocks long and a hundred blocks wide

The Niggers are into the same shit inside—'cept in summer-
time.

A Day in the Life of a Poet

Woke up crying the blues:
bore witness too the sadness of the day;
the peaceful man from Atlanta
was slaughtered yester/day.
Got myself together
drank in the sweetness of sun/shine,
wrote three poems too the peace/ful/lamb
from Atlanta; made love
too a raging Black woman
drank wine
got high: saw angels
leading the lamb too heaven?
the blues gonna get me
gonna get me for sure!
went too the beach/to forget if only eye can
about the gentle soul from Georgia;
ate clam chowder soup and fish sandwiches;
made love in the sand
too this same beautiful woman:
drank in all her sweetness:
lost future child in the sand

saw the bloody sun falling
behind weeping purple clouds;
tears fell in rivers for this gentle lamb
whom eye can't forget.
The bloody star sinking
into the purple grave: blackness falls.
Go out into the decay of day;
copped three keys;
the key of happiness,
the key of creative joy,
the key of sadness.
Came back and watched the gloom on the tube
at her house; which was disrupted.
Kissed her: went home by the route
of the mad speedways: dropped tears in my lap
for the lamb in Atlanta.
Home at last.
Two letters under the door;
a love letter from the past
grips at the roots of memory:
at last another poem published!
good news
during a bad news weekend;
lights out;
drink of grapes;
severed sight close's
another day
in the life.

Flies on Shit

Mah man,
you ever watched
flies on shit?
Ah mean how they gather 'round
and hover hover over
and buzz and buzz and buzz
and then descend into the stink,
into the realness of that stink?!
Ah mean, mah man, have you ever!!
watched a fly eat shit
every day all day long
each and every day
flapping wings
but never ever
flying away for too long?!
him always coming back
too buzz and buzz and buzz
until the stink is there no longer
now its an old turd
brick hard in the sun
now crumbling crumbling
now its falling away too dust
you know, human folks are like that,
always in the shit,
but never ever
flying away;
they always come back
too buzz and buzz
and buzz.

The Wait

all along the rail
road tracks of texas
old train cars lay
rusted and overturned
like new african governments
long forgotten by the people
who built and rode them
till they couldn't run no more,
they remind me of old race horses
who've been put out too pasture
too lay amongst the weeds
rain sleet and snow
till they die and rot away,
they also remind me of fading pictures
in grandma's picture book
of old black men in mississippi
who sit on dreary delapidated porches,
porches that are falling away
like a dead mans skin,
like a white mans eyes,
and on the peeling photos
the old men sit there, sad-eyed
and waiting, waiting for the worms
and the undeniable dust
to come put their claims on them
and they sit there, non-thinking
of the master, and his long forgotten
(even by himself, firstly by himself) promise
of forty acres of landscape
and even now, if you pass across

this bleeding flesh of everchanging
landscape, you will see in the cities,
the stretching countryside
old black men and young black men,
sittin' on porches, waiting,
waiting for the rusted trains
that rot amongst
the texas grass

Dirge

it is the endless dance
of the dead that leads us
too the bleeding songs of the living
soundless footsteps cross eons
of space and resurrections
too greet you here on this morning
without sun, without water, without
life, here where the wind speaks out
but is not heard, where the flames
erupt, but are not felt or seen
the drums have been silenced
but will sing again the beat
of the rhythmic dancers
the conch horn does not call
but will call again the warriors
dancing doo-rags contemplating murder
pimps thinking only of cadillacs

and money will die in the flames of the gutters
and there is no certainty or guarantee
no contract signed by Allah that says
man must reach the twenty-first century
it is the endless soundless dance
of the dead that leads us weeping
too the bleeding crimes of the living
it is the timeless footsteps
of the soundless that speak too us
of the ruin of our heritage

RAYMOND TURNER

Buttons

Buttons: brilliant, beautiful buttons
buttons arouse questions!!
"Free Huey" buttons pose a question of
burning sensation,
What have you done for his liberation??
"B.S.U.-Takin' Care of Business" buttons
ask a question that is vividly clear, How
much have you taken care of this year??
"BLACK POWER" buttons question one's
actual and planned contribution to rea-
lizing the impending revolution.

(an assortment of buttons should be pinned
on Prof. Ken. Clarke's Ass!)

Find a Role, Define a Role

Poems are written by poets for the people
Black music is played by Black Musicians for the
people
Art is created by artists for the people
Prescriptions are prescribed by physicians for the
people

My beautiful Black People with all that soul, each of
you must state and define your role

we need *clerks* who can type; *thieves* who can swipe
we need *barbers* who can style hair; we need *engineers*
who can engineer

we need *scientist, physicist, optimist, romanticist, phy-
sicians, electricians;* we need *dissidents, militants, orators,
intergrators, separators, protestors, investors.*

we need hip niggers from the West as well as East; we
even need niggers to become *police*

. . . . . everybody doin' a thing, an essential particular one,
everybody will inevitably pick up their *gun,* and do his
'thang, bang, bang . . .

JACQUES WAKEFIELD

"it ain't no jive"

it ain't no jive
   dat we return ta ourselves bruthers,
  its fo real dat the beauty of
   ourselves is down pat agin yaknow
though moms calls us crazy we love
dis craziness which is love
     of
   ourselves agin ourselves in
       love
   agin an git a black queen an
      make a son yall

"our world is"

  our world is
   what we make it
make it
   (black soul eyes searching)
  make it
let's make it beautiful
    fo the purpose of peace
 agin our world of love
     agin

black people   rediscover
spiritual things
agin in life!!!   fo our world. back agin fo
the purpose of peace we live. harmonious minds
of peaceful
blackness!!!   BLACK PEOPLE folks
o love people harmonious
agin in our world of love.
we make it strong an keep on gittin up . . .
keep on!   gittin up
an keep on!   gittin up

"well well"

well well
mah ace boo coo
mah mans yall princess
in colony streets   yall   well good gahd!
the world is us now
mah mans us princes
of peace ooo strong Uh!!!
bad spirit black powers well Uh yooknow
our thang now Uh!!!
HEY! mah ace boon
black princess coo
black jitterbug bop hustle sharp man ooooo
tip tip tip uh Hey!! our thang yooknow
hey oo Ow good gahd no jive
(well yooknow) itsblackitsblackitsblack
mah mans fo-ever

DELL WASHINGTON

Learning Family

There they all were:
Aunt Maisy, Aunt Lula, Aunt Bird;
Grandma was one of thirteen
and they all asked about Mattie,
her Grandma. They called her Aunt Mattie.

Then there were the ones
that called her mother aunt:
Sherman Ray, Lola Jean, Son, and Reggie.
All Portia's age,
all her cousins
and all so different.
She was brown, Lola yellow
with red hair and gray eyes,
Sherman Ray black with brown palms
and pink instead of white in his eyes.

All of them her first cousins.
She was an only child.

And the land was different:
acres of hard ground growing sparse brown grass,
huge cows that had horns
and surprised her with mooing
that she didn't think at all friendly.
When she ran she stepped in their dung.

Then over the hill
in the hot sun
to Uncle Losh's where they got
strawberry pop so cold
she was last to finish in all that heat.

Through a barbed wire fence
where the quiet of the woods scared her.
When they played hide and seek
she was it
until they all came out running and laughing.
A bell was clanking off somewhere—
some lost cow they said—
back through the fence and to the tank.
It was a lake.
They didn't say
why they called it the tank.
Her uncle had almost drowned there
one night when he was drunk.
They sat at the edge
until Sherman Ray caught a crayfish
and tried to give it to her.

Way back around a ravine where coachwhip snakes hid.
If one caught you
it would give you a whipping.
Trying to see one and running,
all of them,
as fast as they could
when they saw something move in the ravine

and still she managed to keep up.

Down another hill to the two room houses
when she tripped and fell
to find her face
in a startling blue flower,
a bluebell they said.
They grew in patches together.
She felt the cold
coming up from the well.
Reggie let the bucket drop
all the way to the bottom
to let her hear it.
Then let her wind it up herself
to see what kind of work it was.

Dinner was special:
barbecued spareribs and hot links from Bunnytown
with corn bread and turnip greens
to cool the hot sauce
and red soda water in clear plastic glasses.
The light came from an oil lamp
that was smoky and hot at the top.
Only Bird had electricity.
At the meal
her uncle promised to let her ride the horse
the next day.
After helping to wash the dishes
in a white enameled pan,
they went out into the black
to set off firecrackers.

She waited to see how they did it.

She started each time at the loud explosion.
Finally, lighting one of hers
but no explosion.
Finding it and it went off in her hand.
When she looked
she was amazed to see it whole.
There wasn't even the least bit of blood.

But she just watched

and let them set off the rest.

ALAN WEEKS

Some Brothers Cry

Some brothers cry
REVOLUTION! REVOLUTION!
EQUALITY! FREEDOM NOW!
And sell their sisters
For some cheap red wine high.

Pimping for the no face Honkey,
To get them a cadillac
And a pair of grey pastel alligator shoes
Now they're flying high, feeling fine.

But in the end . . . ?
These brothers wind up in alleys of the Harlems
Of God Bless Amerikkka
And die broken and confused
In their grey pastel alligator shoes.

Yes, we cry REVOLUTION!
And commit Fratricide with a smile.

MICHYLE WHITE

"I prepare for night changes"

I prepare for night changes
With the unbelievable trees
Leaves turned up for the rain

Sexy wind caressing
The nape of my neck
Sliding across my shoulders

All around me there is life
And death is gentle and right
There is nothing to be sad about
Anymore.

ART WILSON

Treasure Hunt
(*The Young Hopefuls*)

Lucky stars are for gazing upon and lying to yourself
    about....
        Things that are about to take place and be
        realized.....

Like when the world explodes you won't be destroyed....
Like when the streets buckle and the cities burn you can
    watch
        It on television.... Along with Captain Midnight
        and—
        Lassie....

Naw! You ain't gonna have it that easy.....
Naw! It ain't gonna leave you behind to lie about how you
    did
        Some good things in your life and God spared
        you.....
Naw! Naw! Naw!

It ain't gon be that way.....
You too were shoveling words and looking for gold
    mines.... With
        Veins that ran through space and time.....
You to were pick axing your way through traditional places
    of

Solitude, composure, and peace. . . . .

And life ran red through the hills of oblivion and
      fiery
Lava did envelop the head of ambition. . . . .
      scorching even
The tasteless-souless entities that resided
      inside. . . . . .

When you wish upon a star, it makes all the difference
      who you
            Are. . . . Foreshadowing illusions of goals yet
                  realized. . . . .
Pipedreams that eat at the core of being and non-
      existence. . . .

Ghetto dwellers wishin' and hopin'. . . . that death over-
      takes life. . . .
            For cop-outs sake. . . . .
Walls that fold to the symmetrical notions of roaches
      crawling
            Back and forth. . . .
Calendars with little significance—except perhaps to count
      the
            Number of hungry days that have passed. . . . .
            Except perhaps to count the days till winter when
                  you'll
            Probably freeze to death. . . .

You know it gits to be a game we play with ourselves. . . .
      like
Russian roulette. . . . only someone else has his finger on
      the

Trigger. . . . and sooner—the nuclear trigger gon be
   pulled and. . . . .

Yes lucky stars often fiend on the gazer perhaps ask-
   ing. . . . .
            "Why look at me. . . . look at yourself. . . . ."
Yes, look at yourself. . . .
Gaze into your soul and pull that hidden ripcord that
   means. . . .
            You're bailing out. . . .
Out of your mind. . . . going inside sanity. . . . insanity. . . .
   Tense
            Feeling that grasps the rims of the world and
               squeezes the
            Bitterness of fruitless thoughts into a cesspool of
               acids
            That submerge the bones of oppressed peoples
               and walk the
            Threads of time. . . .

Bailing out into transliterating fingers of gesticulations—
   Phony—Bogard politicians. . . .
Bailing out into infamous misery of obtuse infinity. . . .
            Lost. . . .

Treasure hunt, your game. . . .
         Hope, your only tool. . . .
            Release, your last step. . . .

Black Sunrise

I.

Oh! Loard remember me!
> Black screams of galleys lay, for dead. . . . boat-
> loads. . . . boats full.

Oh! Loard remember me!
> White curses. . . . scorn of ages. . . . sorrow of
> Blacks. . . .

Wheels of time spin. . . . crazily out of length. . . . and
measure. . . .

Forsaken mothers. . . . fathers. . . . strong and Black. . . .
bought & sold. . . .

Land. . . . forty acres and a mule. . . . lies. . . . for free. . . .
for me. . . .

North and south. . . . east and west. . . . land. . . .
> I only own the dust on my shoes. . . . dust of
> ages. . . . hearts of stones. . . .

Pyramids. . . . amid. . . . the sands of ages. . . . sands of
me. . . .

Egyptians spears in land. . . . once owned. . . . Many a tear
ago. . . .
> Crying pleas of let alone. . . . fall to winds. . . .
> hearts of stone. . . .
> Pride, dignity, culture—gone. . . . away. . . .

Oh! Loard remember me! Yes, Jesus loves me. . . .
> Chains and shackles. . . . holding fast. . . . I can't
> last. . . . I can't last. . . .
> Charred bodies. . . . feathered and tarred. . . . I can't
> last. . . . I can't last. . . .
> > Yes, Jesus loves me. . . .

Oh! Loard remember me!
    Uncle Tom. . . . and Tomeline. . . . have yet to see
        what I've seen. . . .
                Seen enough. . . . seen enough. . . .
    Black. . . . senators. . . . judges. . . . postal clerks. . . .
        progress 1875—
                Seen enough. . . . seen enough. . . .
    Walk-a-run past lynch-a-niggah-tree. . . . you've yet
        to see. . . . yet to see. . . .
    Jim Crow trucks-it-on-in. . . . don't you see. . . .
        don't ya'—

Oh! Loard remember me! Nobody knows the trouble I
see—
    Search for a new land. . . . search for a black
        man. . . . castrated. . . . castrated. . . .
            Sold my soul to the white man's store. . . .
    Found. . . . agony. . . . pain. . . . distress. . . . and
        lies. . . . and my man. . . .
                castrated. . . . castrated. . . .

Ear drums beat by air vibrations say. . . .
        A change gone come. . . . it came for Sam. . . .
Sam Cooke. . . . who used to cook in his own right. . . .
    right. . . .
        Understand me. . . .
Race of shadows. . . . town of spooks. . . . morbid, there I
    do. . . .
Bequeath. . . . to you. . . .
I pass the baton. . . . the baton of civil rights to you. . . .
    tired. . . . tired
Of runnin' in circles. . . . done lost the track. . . .

Always losin' time on curves. . . . gradualism. . . . wait. . . .
Enter the hope peddler. . . . with a gift of nature. . . .
you hip to it. . . .

II.

Shoop. . . . shoobee. . . . doo da-day papa. . . . soux. . . .
Do your thing fella, 'cause if you don't I will. . . .
Clocks. . . . with hands of the dead and living, clasp across
the space of time. . . .
Expensive, gold plated. . . . shock resistant. . . . water
proofed. . . . wrist watches. . . .
Expensive, mohair, alpaca sweaters. . . . and silk suits. . . .
stingy brims. . . .
Diamond stickpins and alligator shoes. . . . glistening in
the sun. . . . sunrise. . . .

Harbari gani dada na ndugu. . . .

Ethno-centric. . . . song of ages. . . . tune of us. . . .

Oh! Shango. . . . god of torture. . . . drink of my life. . . .
taste the bitter
Grapes of wrath. . . . raisin, me. . . .
Jungle. . . . vineyards. . . . tumble weed. . . . no starting
blocks. . . . for Blacks. . . .

Shallow words echo through the channel of my breath. . . .
borrowed breath. . . .
Not much left. . . . not much left. . . .
Finger-poppin', no money shoppin', street walkin', fast
talkin', cigarette
Smokin'. . . . piece totin'. . . . brothers. . . . hustler by
trade. . . . mutant by choice. . . .

Yes, I dig marvel comic books!
  And spiderman and antman are both niggahs. . . .
    who else could communicate
With bugs that well. . . . except someone who done
    lived with them all
    His life. . . . And Captain America never loses his
      red, white, and blue. . . .
                    Salimu. . . . Salimu. . . .

III.

Rock my soul in the bosom of JOB—tipping. . . . causa-
tion. . . . havoc. . . . running down alleys of shadowed
people. . . . turning corners on two wheels. . . . a wheel of
mind and a wheel of emotion. . . . churnin' the butter of
melted. . . . wasted lives. . . . wasted over vats of cess-
pools. . . . where ghetto children baptize themselves. . . .
in crime. . . . punishment. . . . and desperation. . . .
super spade. . . . turned green with money of liberal
castes. . . . Brahmins—diggin'—the untouchables—India-
colored ghetto. . . . 1968. . . . revised hard-back edition. . . .

Nicotine fits and junkie strikes. . . . war fasts and time
    bombs—set
To go off in the sun months. . . . sunshine. . . .
Dark nights. . . . light as day. . . . lit up with flames of
    pre-empted
Self-defense. . . . If the black go—so do you. . . . violence.
    . . . death. . . .
Violence. . . . fixed. . . . junkie strikes out. . . . punching
    time cards, cause you
Were off yo' job. . . . yo' job. . . . yo' job. . . .

Your country, yes indeed. . . . waste land of slavery
On it I scream
Land where brothers are lynched, land where slave-boats
were sent. . . .
From every voice dissent. . . . let freedom ring.

Radio free. . . . stereo-freeze. . . . sounds of clashing
tarnished dreams. . . .
Sandman playing Napoleon with bedroom stereotypes. . . .
bushy-tailed girls
With sweaty sweaters and too much make-up. . . . make
up my life. . . .

Who am I? I'm Captain Midnight, master of the universe,
and psycho rolled into a joint. . . . with licorice brown
papers. . . . I'm Jim Crow. . . . the impeccable. . . I'm
steppin'-fetchit—still steppin' and fetchin'—I'm the Kingfish
tryin to beat Andy, my brother, out of some money. . . .
I'm tellin' tales on Uncle Remus that can't be taught. . . .
not in his back yard. . . . the ghetto. . . . I'm Hansel with
Gretel looking for nirvana. . . . I'm Booker T. Washington
lookin' out for white interests. . . . and I'm Simon Legree—
'cause Uncle Tom won the war and bitter grapes. . . .
don't git ripe—until sunrise. . . . and for us Black grapes—
a Black sunrise. . . .

IV.

Sunrise of Blacks. . . . the ghetto light. . . . a promethean
flame of
Warmth in being. . . . learning life first hand—never gittin'
another

Shuffle of the cards—cards of you. . . .
Unity with yourself alone. . . . flew and passed your
    window pane—
Close the shades of your eyes—do not discover the
    light. . . . 'tis sunrise. . . .

The setting of the sun four centuries ago. . . . tells the
    tale. . . .
Peering through portholes with the rats. . . . blacks saw
    the sun set

So many years ago. . . .
And now at last sunrise for the people of darkness. . . .
sunrise for the people of dispossession. . . . sunrise for an
extra-culture. . . . sunrise. . . . sunrise. . . .
        Black sunrise. . . .

AL YOUNG

I Arrive in Madrid

The wretched of the earth
are my brothers.
Neither priest
nor state
nor state of mind
is all God is
who must understand
to have put up for so long
with my drinking & all my restlessness
my hot & cold running around
unwired
to any dogma;
the way I let the eyes
of dark women
in southern countries
rock my head
like a translucent vessel
in turbulent waters.

Long have I longed for adventure,
a peculiar kind of romance
on the high seas of this planet.
Victimized at last
I float alone
exploring time
in search of tenderness

a love
with no passage attached.

So this is dictatorship,
a watery monday morning
smell of the atlantic
still blowing thru me.
If you have ever died or been born
you will understand
when I speak of everything being salty
like the taste of my mama's tears
when I came back to earth
thru her
after so much of the bombing & blood-letting
had taken place here
when Spain was the name of some country
she'd heard tell of from the words of a popular song
publicized over the radio.

This city too
feels as tho it's held together by publicity
but publicity is going to lose its power
over the lives of men
once we have figured out just what within us
is more powerful & more beautiful
than program or text.

For now
there is language & Spanish to cope with,
there are eyelashes & chromosomes
pesetas pounds francs & dollars
& a poverty even wine cannot shut out.

Dancing on the Shore

Like the clever seagull
who snacks all day long
I too was born to be near water

Ocean Springs, Mississippi
New Orleans
Detroit
Chicago
New York
San Francisco
Lisbon
Lake Chapala, Jalisco
—the story of my life
told
blindfold

I yearn to go
where the waters go

I love to go walking
& pass the time
hovering out over the water

For Poets

Stay beautiful
but don't stay down underground too long
Don't turn into a mole
or a worm
or a root
or a stone

Come on out into the sunlight
Breathe in trees
Knock out mountains
Commune with snakes
& be the very hero of birds

Don't forget to poke your head up
& blink
Think
Walk all around
Swim upstream

Don't forget to fly

Moon-Watching by Lake Chapala

> "I love to cross a river in very
> bright moonlight and see the
> trampled water fly up in chips
> of crystal under the oxen's feet."
> —The Pillow Book of Sei Shonagon,
> 10th Century
> (transl: Arthur Waley)

IT CAN BE beautiful this sitting by oneself all alone
except for the world, the very world a literal extension of
living leaf, surface & wave of light: the moon for example.
American poet Hazel Hall felt,
> "I am less myself
> & more of the sun"
> which I think

upon these cool common nights being at some remove, in spirit at least, from where they are busy building bombs & preparing concentration camps to put my people into; I am still free to be in love with dust & limbs (vegetable & human) & with lights in the skies of high spring.

IN THE AFTERNOON you watch fishermen & fisherboys in mended boats dragging their dark nets thru the waters. You can even buy a little packet of dried sardines like I do, a soda, & lean against the rock & iron railings but you won't be able to imagine the wanderings of my own mustachio'd dad who was a fisherman in Mississippi in the warm streams of the Gulf of Mexico. How time loops & loops! Already I'm drunk with the thought of distances. I do that look skyward & re-chart the constellations. No one to drop in on. No one to drop in on me. It's been a long time since I've had nothing better to do than establish myself in one spot & stare directly into the faces of the moon, the golden orange white brown blue moon, & listen to the tock of my heart slowing down in the silence. I can almost hear in the breeze & picture in the sniffable award-winning moonlight the doings & dyings of my hardworking father, of all my heartbroken mamas & dads.

WHO WILL LIVE to write The Role of Moonlight in the Evolution of Consciousness?

IN NEW YORK, San Francisco & points in between the sad young men & women are packaging their wounds & hawking them; braggadocios cleansing old blood from syringes & sly needles in preparation for fresh offerings of

cold hard chemical bliss; ofays wasted on suburban pleni-
tude; not-together Bloods strung out on dreams.

I'M OUT HERE alone, off to one side, in the soft dark
inspecting a stripe of tree shadow on my moonlit hand,
dissolving into mineral light, quivering donkey light, the
waters churning with fish & flora, happiness circulating
thru my nervous system like island galaxies thru space.

*   *   *

MEXICO CAN BE Moon can be Madness can be Maya.
But the rising notion that we are in the process of evolving
from ape to angel under the influence of star-gazing is the
Dream.

Dancing All Alone

We move thru rooms & down the middle of freeways,
myself & I.
A feeling lumps up in the throat
that says I won't be living forever.
The middle of the month signifies
the end of some beginning
the beginning of some end.
Once I thought the heart could be ripped out
like doll filling
& naked essence examined
but I'm a man
not a manikin.

I would transfer to the world
my idea of what it's like beneath flesh & fur.
I cannot do this without making fools of myself.
Cold winds whoosh down on me under winter stars
& the way ahead is long but not uncertain.
I am neither prince nor citizen
but I do know what is noble in me
& what is usefully vulgar.
It is from this point that the real radiates.
I move & am moved,
do & am done for.
My prison is the room of myself
& my rejection of both is my salvation,
the way out being the way in,
the freeway that expands to my true touch,
a laughter in the blood that dances.

A Dance for Militant Dilettantes

No one's going to read
or take you seriously,
a hip friend advises,
until you start coming down on them
like the black poet you truly are
& ink in lots of black in your poems
soul is not enough
you need real color
shining out of real skin

nappy snaggly afro hair
baby grow up & dig on *that!*

You got to learn to put in about
stone black fists
coming up against white jaws
& red blood splashing
down those fabled wine & urine-
stained hallways
black bombs blasting out real white estate
the sky itself black with what's to come:
final holocaust
the settling up

Don't nobody want no nice nigger no more
these honkies man that put out
these books & things
they want an angry splib
a furious nigrah
they don't want no bourgeois woogie
they want them a militant nigger
in a fiji haircut
fresh out of some secret boot camp
with a bad book in one hand
& a molotov cocktail in the other
subject to turn up at one of their conferences
or soirees
& shake the shit out of them

The Move Continuing

All beginnings start right here.
The suns & moons of our spirits
keep touching.
I look out the windows at rain
& listen casually to latest developments
of the apocalypse
over the radio
barely unpacked
& hear you shuttling in the background
from one end of the new apartment
to the other
bumping into boxes of personal belongings
I can barely remember having touched 48 hours ago.
Jazz
a very ancient music
whirls beneficently
into our rented front room,
Coltrane blessing us with a loving presence.
I grow back thru years
to come upon myself
shivering
in my own presence.
That was a long time ago
when the bittersweet world
passed before
(rather than thru)
me
a vibratory collage
of delights
in supercolor.

It wasn't difficult becoming a gypsy.
At one end of the line
there was God
& at the very other end
there is God.
In between
shine all the stars of all the spaces
illuminating everything
to the two tender points
that are your eyes,
the musical instruments
of these strong but gentle black men
glowing in the dark,
the darkness of my own heart
beating its way along
thru all the evenings
that lengthen my skies,
all the stockings
that have ever been rolled down
sadly,
lover & beloved
reaching
to touch one another
at this different time
in this different place
as tho tonight were only the beginning
of all those
yester-
days.

BIOGRAPHIES OF POETS

S. E. ANDERSON: Born August 16, 1943, in Bedford-Stuyvesant. Went to Lincoln University, Pa. and did grad work in Mathematics. Teacher by profession. U.S. editor of the *New African Magazine* (London), co-editor of *MOJO, Black Dialogue;* on the Advisory Board of Drum and Spear Press. Have contributed frequently to *Negro Digest, Journal of Black Poetry, Black Culture Weekly;* in the *Black Fire* anthology (eds. Jones and Neal) and the Clarence Major anthology: *New Black Poets.* Presently teaching Harlem adults elementary Algebra.

DESIRÉE A. BARNWELL: (Mrs. Lawrence S. Cumberbatch): Lives and works in the metropolitan New York area. Born in Guyana, South America and raised and educated in New York City, she holds a B.A. in Sociology from Queens College. "Will the Real Black People Please Stand" is her first published work.

JOSEPH BEVANS BUSH: Born in Philadelphia, Pa. and educated in the public school system of that city. He has been writing for approximately fifteen years and is a member of The Philadelphia Writers Club. His poems and articles have appeared in *Negro Digest, Liberator, The Philadelphia Tribune, Pride Magazine, The Negro History Bulletin, Philly Talk* and *The Philadelphia Independent. Black Arts: An Anthology of Black Creations* has published one of his poems. His work appears in two other books: *A Galaxy of Black Writing* and *Contemporary American Negro Poets, 1970.*

PEARL CLEAGE: Born December 7, 1948, Springfield, Mass. Lived for fifteen years in Detroit, Michigan. Attended Howard University for three years. Now married and working at the Martin Luther King, Jr. Memorial Center in Atlanta, Georgia.

JAYNE CORTEZ: Comes from Los Angeles, California. Her poems have appeared in *Black Dialogue* and *Negro Digest.* "How Long Has Trane Been Gone?" and "For Real" are from her collection of poetry: *Pisstained Stairs and the Monkey Man's Wares,* published by Phrase Text.

STANLEY CROUCH: Born, 1945 in Los Angeles. He teaches literature, black drama and music appreciation through the Black Studies Center of the Claremont Colleges, California. He plays mean drums and is the bandleader of Stanley Crouch and the Black Music Infinity. His recording of poetry, *Ain't No Ambulances for No Niggahs Tonight* can be heard on Flying Dutchman Records.

LAWRENCE S. CUMBERBATCH: Presently a student in law school, I am a by-product of the New York City Public Schools and a graduate of Queens College. I was born in Brooklyn in 1946 and gained consciousness in 1962.

WALTER K. DANCY:
Born in April 24, 1946 (Taurus)
fourth of eight children
Father played guitar and sang blues
Mother an excellent story-teller
Neither finished grade school
I feel that life is music given flesh. All life interest—pain, beauty, struggle
Imagination is most real for seeing possibilities that limited reality excludes.
Am curious to understand the entire universe and mirror it in poetry.

JACKIE EARLEY: Was born in Buffalo, adopted and raised in Cambridge, Ohio. Ran away from home at seventeen. Homesteaded in Cleveland, Ohio. Regained the consciousness that was lost at birth. Went to the South for a year working hard. Now living in New York and hardly working. Studies philosophy and plans to retrace by boat the way back to Africa via the old slave route. Right on for my people!

MARI EVANS: A native of Toledo, Ohio, was a John Hay Whitney Fellow, 1965-66. Her work as a poet has been used on record albums, several television specials, two off-Broadway productions and over thirty textbooks and anthologies, including Italian, German, Swedish, British, French and Dutch works. Presently Writer-in-Residence at Indiana University-Purdue University, Indianapolis, she is also producer/director of a weekly half-hour television series "The Black Experience."

LANON A. FENNER, JR.: This young poet lives in New York City.

WALLY FORD: Significantly enough I was born on a Friday the thirteenth in New York City, January 1950. Since then, my total direction and training, as first provided by my parents, and now by myself as well, has been dedicated towards attacking those who would wreak havoc on the symbolism of Black meaning and make death a reality. My attack has not been sucessful to date, but I am still trying, and that is what I am all about. I am also a student at Dartmouth College, but soon that will be in the past. My poems are to express those things to Black people which I feel need to be said, and, if I succeed in some small way in doing this, then I have begun the attack of which I spoke. And that, simply is what all of this is about.

JANICE MARIE GADSDEN: Born Dec. 8, 1952, in Harlem U.S.A. I grew up in Woodside, New York City in a home where if someone called you Nigger you had to hit them as hard as you could, and if someone called you a black so and so you were supposed to make them say black with respect. In '63 we moved to Springfield Gardens. From 7-12th grade I was one of the few token blacks in the term at Hunter College High School, then in '67 I founded what became the Black Society; and I was president of that society from '68-'69. Presently I am an upper form freshman at Queens College, I am poetry editor of *Whereas* the Queens College literary magazine. Some of my poems have appeared in *Whereas*. I will probably major in English.

PAULA GIDDINGS: Born in Yonkers, New York, now resides in New York City. She is a graduate of Howard University where she edited *The Afro-American Review*, its literary magazine, for three years. This is the first publication of her poetry outside of the Washington, D. C. area.

NIKKI GIOVANNI: Born 1943, Knoxville, Tenn. Graduated Fisk University 1967. Teaching at Livingston College Rutgers University. Presently live with my son in New York City.

CLAY GOSS: Born Clayton Goss—Gemini 5/26/46 in North Philly, Pa. Married to a beautiful Black JUJU woman, Linda and have a daughter, Aisha. Presently attending Howard University where I have had a play of mine *HOMECOOKIN'* produced in the Ira Aldridge Theater. A children's book entitled: *Bill Pickett: Black Bulldogger,* has been published by Hill and Wang. I am dedicated to The Black Liberation of Truth and believe that Tomorrow will be the Soul Soulution, Time the Element of SPACE.

LINDA GOSS: Born Linda McNear—Leo 8/18/47 in Alcoa, Tennessee. Graduated from Howard University in 1969. Beautifully married to Clay Goss and have a happy baby, Aisha. Black Women should color the earth with green fertility, taking care of the "HOMECOOKIN'" while their BLACK Men conquer the OUTSIDE.

DONALD GREEN: Is a twenty-three year old actor-playwright-poet. He has been published in the newspaper, *Forty Acres and A Mule* and featured on WABC's "Like It Is." His poems and plays have been performed by the Har-You Act Drama Unit. As an actor he has appeared in Archie Shepp's *Revolution* and is a recipient of Har-You Act's Best Actor Award.

R. ERNEST HOLMES: Born in Harlem, July 24, 1943, while Blacks were battling police in the streets over the rumored shooting of a Black soldier. Made the early life rounds in Hell's Kitchen, the Lower East Side and Harlem with a view from low-income housing projects. Celloed my way into and out of the High School of Music and Art. Graduate of NYU and NYU School of Law. I have always been awed by the power of The Word and the poetry of the streets.

ALICIA L. JOHNSON: Born February 27, 1944. Author of privately printed book of poems *Realities Vs. Spirits*, other poems have appeared in the following magazines: *Journal* of *Black Poetry, Negro Digest, Nine Black Poets, The New Black Poetry, Présence Africaine* ♯66 & ♯68, *Grassroots, Nommo, Black Expressions, KA,* etc.

CHARLES JOHNSON: Born December 15, 1949
in the land of definitive insanity,
    (Capitalism and the South),
Migrated West,
    to be acculturated and nurtured
On Liberal Southern California Neurosis,
    Trapped 43rd place in black psychosis,
Under this history of life,
    I await the Messiah of black sanity,
Again in the hole,
    of the old South

HERSCHELL JOHNSON: Born in Birmingham, Ala., 1948. Student at Dartmouth. A black poet talks to his people. His spirit/life messages are all about and all around the black world. Black poetry is a life force. It is putting the pressure where it should be. And keeping it there. It is instruction. It is experience. It is an experience. It is movement. It is life. It is a desire for life. It is an indictment against all evil towards black people. It is love just as surely as it is AR/15.

ALICE H. JONES: This poet lives in Buffalo, New York.

ARNOLD KEMP: Was bred in the streets of Harlem, New York. A high school dropout at fifteen, he traveled and knocked around from one dead-end to another. He is presently attending Queens College, New York, as an English major. Aside from his poetry, Mr. Kemp has a produced play: *White Wound, Black Scar,* and is currently wrapping up the last pages of a novel.

JEWEL C. LATIMORE: (JOHARI AMINI): Born in Philadelphia, Pa. and resident of Chicago since childhood. Attended Chicago City College, University of Chicago, Chicago State College (B.A. 1970); published two volumes of poetry *Images in Black* and *Black Essence;* in preparation—a third volume, Spring, 1970; work published in *Black Expression, Journal of Black Poetry, Negro Digest, Nommo, Jump Bad, Pan-African Journal;* member of Organization of Black American Culture (OBAC), and Gwendolyn Brooks's Writers' Workshop.

DON L. LEE: Poet, Essayist, Critic is currently a lecturer in Afro-American Literature and Writer-in-Residence at Northeastern Illinois State College in Chicago. He formerly held the same position at Cornell University, Ithaca, New York. He is also currently serving as lecturer in Afro-American Literature at the University of Illinois, Chicago Circle Campus. He is also a book reviewer for *Negro Digest* and has published three volumes of poetry—*Think Black, Black Pride* and *Don't Cry, Scream,* all published by Broadside Press of Detroit, Michigan. His lecturing and poetry readings have included many colleges and universities in and out of the United States. With Miss Gwendolyn Brooks he took part in the International Poetry Forum in 1968 in Pittsburgh, Pennsylvania. He's currently completing a book of criticism on black poets of the sixties. His work has appeared in *Negro Digest, The Journal of Black Poetry, Evergreen Review, The New York Times, Muhammed Speaks, Freedomways, Liberator, Free Lance, Nommo, The Chicago Daily Defender, Ebony,* etc. His new book, *We Walk the Way of the New World* will appear in February, 1970, published by Broadside Press.

TENA LOCKETT: Born Pittsburg, California, 1945. My mother was my inspiration. Took us on fourteen city block hikes to the Central Libary no matter how cold it was. We read, told stories to each other, felt each other's warmth. Graduated from Southern Illinois University. I teach linguistics and writing at Fisk University, Nashville, Tennessee.

JAMES R. LUCAS: Born in Falmouth, Virginia, a small town across the river from Fredericksburg where I graduated from Walker Grant High School. A graduate of Howard University, my work has appeared in *Negro Digest* and *For Malcolm,* which was published by Broadside Press. I am at present employed by the U. S. Government (P. O.) and reside in Baltimore, Md. with my wife and three children.

BOB MAXEY: Professionally works in manpower development and training; has long been interested in the creative possibilities—and challenges—found in the poetic medium. Intellectually, his concepts have been largely shaped by the Black Man's social and moral condition growing out of the turbulent America of the 60's. Technically, he has sought to distill and refine these highly complex events in the most elemental language and basic cadences possible. To somehow find and state through his poetry the ennobling influences hidden amid the absurdity and violence of our times remains his greatest ambition as a writer.

DON A. MIZELL: Age 21, Aries-Taurus. Point of origin: Fort Lauderdale, Florida, Swarthmore College '71, major: Black Existential Revolution, minor: Anthropology and Political Science. Quickly or so it seems, I traversed kindergarten (first bump, first hump), elementary school (first love?), junior high school (poverty, puberty, and poetry), high school (All-American super nigger), and college (awareness and convergence of Blackness and Cosmic Consciousness). Note to us black folks: transcendence or immanence, take your pick, but be sure to find some *true* connections, e.g. Love.

A. X. NICHOLAS: Born in Mobile, Ala., in 1943. Graduate of Tuskegee Institute. Presently teaching in Detroit Public Schools. Has published in *Negro Digest* and *Chelsea Magazine*. Completing a book of poems to be published in a year or two.

RAYMOND R. PATTERSON: Born in New York City and grew up on Long Island, which somewhat accounts for my becoming a poet. Lincoln University, Pa., and New York University gave me time to think and a way of making a living. An incomplete disillusionment with life, an extraordinary wife and a daughter named Ama account for the rest of it.

ARTHUR PFISTER: Born in New Orleans, September 1949. Trying to be like a hip white boy, I ran away from home at the age of eighteen and met Sam Allen a year later at Tuskegee Institute where I started writing poems . . . I want to continue.

HERBERT LEE PITTS: A twenty-one-year-old native from Baltimore, Maryland's lesser known "Harlem." Since 1965 he has worked with the Student Non-violent Co-ordinating Committee (this committee is presently The Student Coordinating Committee) and the Black Panther Party. In 1968 he attended Tuskegee Institute, where he helped organize the Student Organization for Black Unity. His political activities led to his arrest, conviction and subsequent sentencing to eight years in a federal penitentiary, where he is presently incarcerated pending an appeal.

TIMOTHY L. PORTER: Born, 1946 in Woodstock, Maryland. He is a graduate of Holy Cross College, and is now studying law at New York University. Mr. Porter plans to continue writing, and hopes to contribute to the development of more responsive social institutions in this country.

ERIC PRIESTLEY: Born December 16, 1943, one of four children. He graduated from Jefferson High School, then attended East Los Angeles College, majoring in English. He received his degree in Psychology in March 1970 from California State College, Los Angeles College. Was active in the Watts Writer's Workshop and Studio Watts. His poem *Can You 'Dig Where I'm Coming From* appeared in *Watts Poets* edited by Quincy Troupe. Presently he's working on a novel *God Is the Sun,* about the Watts writers.

T. L. ROBINSON: Born, July 6, 1946, small Mississippi town, was accutely aware very early of Jim Crow. Moved to Palo Alto, California, at fifteen became aware of Malcolm's warning: "As long as you're south of the Canadian Border you're South." Graduated from Stanford University, 1969. Presently working with Urban Institute at Montclair State College, New Jersey.

CAROLYN M. RODGERS: (IMANI): Born and raised in dirty Chicago. I majored in English and Psychology in college and somehow managed not to learn anything but what I wanted to learn. I have been a social worker all of my working years.

I play the guitar and I love to sing, almost as much as I love to write. I have ben writing *seriously* for three years. Now I have been writing since the age of nine, but seriously, that's another matter. I want to write a novel and at least one good play. I want to utimately write like Smokey sings. Or 'Trane plays. I have also taught Afro-American Literature.

SONIA SANCHEZ: blk/woman/mother/poet/teacher/barely surviving in wite/assed/amurica.

RUBY C. SAUNDERS: Of Alexandria, Virginia, attended Hampton Institute in Hampton, Virginia. Received a Bachelor of Science degree in Chemistry and Mathematics. Attended Howard University as a graduate student in Organic Chemistry. Came to New York City as a chemist for the Federal Government in 1967. After joining the Negro Ensemble Company's Playwright's Workshop decided to leave the scientific field and enter the Theatre full time as dancer, playwright, actress, and poet. Miss Saunders has danced professionally with the Modern Dance Council of Washington, D.C., with the Howard Players, and the Recreation Department of Washington, D.C. and New York City. Since coming to New York, Miss Saunders has appeared in and written several plays. She has also written a collection of poems entitled *American Born Black,* from which the following poems were chosen.

JOHNIE SCOTT: Is Presently attending Stanford University, working for a B.A. in Creative Writing. He plans to continue his education at Stanford's School of Communications, Broadcasting and Film. He is a Research Assistant at Stanford and works under St. Clair Drake in the Afro and Afro-American Studies Program there. He is also a Co-Director of the Black Studies Workshop in Creative Writing at Stanford.

SAUNDRA SHARP: A native of Cleveland, is the author of a volume of poetry, *From The Windows Of My Mind,* and writes primarily "for the pleasure and challenge of creating." As a professional actress-singer she played "Prissy" in Gordon Parks' *The Learning Tree,* and performed on and off Broadway in *Hello, Dolly!, To Be Young, Gifted and Black, Black Quartet,* etc., and did her first public readings with Poets and Performers. She heads Togetherness Productions, a theatrical company established to stage the works of black creative artists.

DAN SIMMONS: Began writing poetry during the turbulent summer of 1963. He has contributed poetry to *The Amsterdam News, The NAACP Journal, The Moonlight Review, Pace Press* and *Negro Digest.* Dan Simmons received his B.A. and M.A. degrees from Howard University. Currently he is District Supervisor of the West Side High School Districts in Manhattan, and an Adjutant Assistant Professor at Pace College, where he teaches Black History and Black Culture.

SHIRLEY STAPLES: A nineteen-year-old junior majoring in English at Tuskegee Institute, Alabama. Born in Bessemer, Alabama. Most of her poetry has previously been published in issues of *The Campus Digest* and other student newspaper publications.

GLENN STOKES: This young poet lives in New York City.

ROBERT L. TERRELL: Twenty-six, is a freelance writer and student in the Graduate School of Journalism at the University of California at Berkeley. He graduated from Morehouse College in June, 1969 and has worked as a general assignment reporter for *The New York Post.* His articles have appeared in *Commonweal, Eye, The Guardian, Negro Digest* and *Evergreen Review.*

CHARLES THOMAS: Rose from the red clay of Oklahoma (McAlester). Implanted with seeds of blackness from Toussaint L'-Ouverture High School, continued at Langston University with poet Melvin B. Tolson. Made westward flight to San

Francisco State College. Labored for the cause with the Afro-American Folkloric Troup. May be found in New York doing his thing on stage and screen (Screen Actors Guild). Dancing Rhythms of Black Life (Chuck Davis Dance Company). Singing songs of the ancestors (on L.P. "Egbe Ommo Nago"). Challenging young minds (Lefferts Jr. High School). Pursuing knowledge (Brooklyn College Graduate School). Directing music ("The Missa Liba") and writing poetry as long as there is something to say.

JAMES W. THOMPSON: Born December 21, 1935. Traveler through schools of thought and a Fascistic system predicated on "skin-colored" economic and political realities—the historical delusion. Attended the necessary schools—several colleges— Wayne State, University of Detroit, University of Alaska. From the destroyed but none broken home: my father was killed in World War II, his love we lost. My mother, an incredible beauty, and two aunts attended my becoming. Professional dancer: Sada Gerard & Co., Melvin Jones & Co., Clifford Fears & Co. (Stockholm, Sweden), amateur photographer, choreographed Ice Show for Alaskan Winter Carnival, 1955. Published in various periodicals and anthologies; volume of early poems: *First Fire* scheduled for Spring 1970 publication, Paul Breman, Ltd., London, England. Presently at work on a volume of short stores entitled *Aint No Love* and a long overdue novel.

QUINCY TROUPE: Born July 23, 1943, in New York City. Raised in St. Louis, Missouri. Attended Grambling College; went into the army for two years, then to Los Angeles and U.C.L.A. studying Journalism. Edited a magazine called *Shrewd,* an anthology called *Watts Poets & Writers,* which will be publblished in March by New Directions Publishing House. My poem *Ode to John Coltrane* will appear in the annual year end big issue of *Downbeat* magazine, I have also read my work on national television. I am married and teach Comparative Literature at Ohio University in Athens, Ohio.

RAYMOND TURNER: Born in San Pedro, California, twenty-one years ago. I was inspired to write by the violent death of comrade Thomas "Lil Tommy" Lewis, a lieutenant of the Black Panther Party, August 5, 1968. Prior to writing poetry I had been writing political satire for a local Black owned newspaper, *The Herald Dispatch*. I am a student at Cal State, Los Angeles. I have done numerous readings at California colleges where I am known as "The People's Poet" for the manner in which my poetry relates to the people through the use of concrete, identifiable objects, instead of abstract similes and metaphors.

JACQUES WAKEFIELD: Actor-poet-singer, bred in Harlem, emphasizes that the pieces enclosed within are "reflecting a life style of boss spirits in our existence." I am a member now of the National Black Theatre, where most of my learning concerning the realms of Black American life has been attained. I have been published in *Journal of Black Poetry* and *Black Fire*, an anthology edited by LeRoi Jones and Larry Neal. Besides being a part of the National Black Theatre's stage productions, I also had the opportunity to do television programs, such as "Black Heritage," "CBS Repertory Workshop" and "Soul."

DELL WASHINGTON: B.A. from Stanford. Had stories published in the Stanford *Sequoia* and *Black on Black* of which she was also an associate editor. Presently enrolled at Yale Law School.

ALAN WEEKS: 22, Born in the ghetto of Brooklyn, New York. Here he had his baptism in the dangerous waters of being black in America. In addition to being a psychology student (City College of New York) and poet, Mr. Weeks pursues a full-time theatrical career. He seeks the liberation of Black people. He wants to capture—on film, on stage, in his poetry—his people's awareness of their beauty.

MICHYLE WHITE: Is twenty years old and lives in New York. She wrote this poem when she was nineteen.

ART WILSON: I grew up on the streets of Southern California, or more specifically Watts. And, like a lot of brothers that grew up in the Watts of America, I found a need to communicate to myself and my people—the/my form for this has been poetry. Born in San Diego, California, attended Fremont High School in L.A., and now attends Stanford University—majoring in Political Science, minoring in Afro-American Studies. Age twenty-two. I worked with the Watts Writers' Workshop, and Budd Schulberg, before I came to the Bay Area, where I am now involved with the Stanford Black Writers' Workshop and Afro-West (Black Cultural Organization).

AL YOUNG: Born 1939, Ocean Springs, Mississippi; reared near there and in Detroit; began writing at age nine, composing detective, western and science fiction stories in nickel school notebooks. Wrote radio scripts in seventh grade and also published my own ditto'd humor magazine, *The Krazy Krazette*. Edited the campus literary magazine *Generation* at the University of Michigan (Ann Arbor)—educated there and at the University of California, Berkeley, concentrating in Spanish. Have traveled all over the United States, Mexico and Southern Europe. Have also worked as professional musician as well as disc jockey, railyard clerk for the S.P., lab assistant, contruction worker, medical photographer, edit the review *Loveletter*. Corinth Books, New York, brought out my first book of poetry *Dancing* in 1969; Holt, Rinehart and Winston published my novel *Snakes* in 1970; am presently working on two new books, one of them a novel set in the San Francisco Bay Area, called *Who Is Angelina?*